# Praise for *Influencing Today's Youth*

Debut author Hughes writes of "transforming the world," via better communication with children.

Once an unwed teen mother herself, now a Ph.D. running a behavioral health center, Hughes writes frankly about how to discuss and model appropriate behavior on tough topics that routinely baffle both adults and children: obesity, education, sex and, above all, learning from mistakes.

Her approach is simple, direct and honest. "If we don't talk about [sex], our kids will find a way to talk about it anyway," she writes, urging the reader to take the path of greatest benefit instead of least resistance. But discussing those tough topics with young people doesn't mean treating them as adults. "They're going to be adults soon enough. Let them be kids while they can. In fact, insist upon it," Hughes states. She reinforces the importance of connection and social responsibility with interviews of other community-centered professionals, occasionally punctuating her points with stories of extraordinary individuals who've chosen to step up and make a difference in a young person's life.

Hughes has a knack for reducing complicated concepts to their basic principles, as when she explains that "influencing" kids boils down to being present, open and acting responsibly. She's a strong voice speaking from within the community—not standing apart—to reassure readers that they're in a position to do real good, right now. "Children, especially young children, learn through observation," Hughes writes, reinforcing the importance of owning one's own actions. "Your words have value, but not as much value as your actions."

Hughes' straightforward, honest approach makes potentially intimidating topics manageable.

—KIRKUS REVIEW

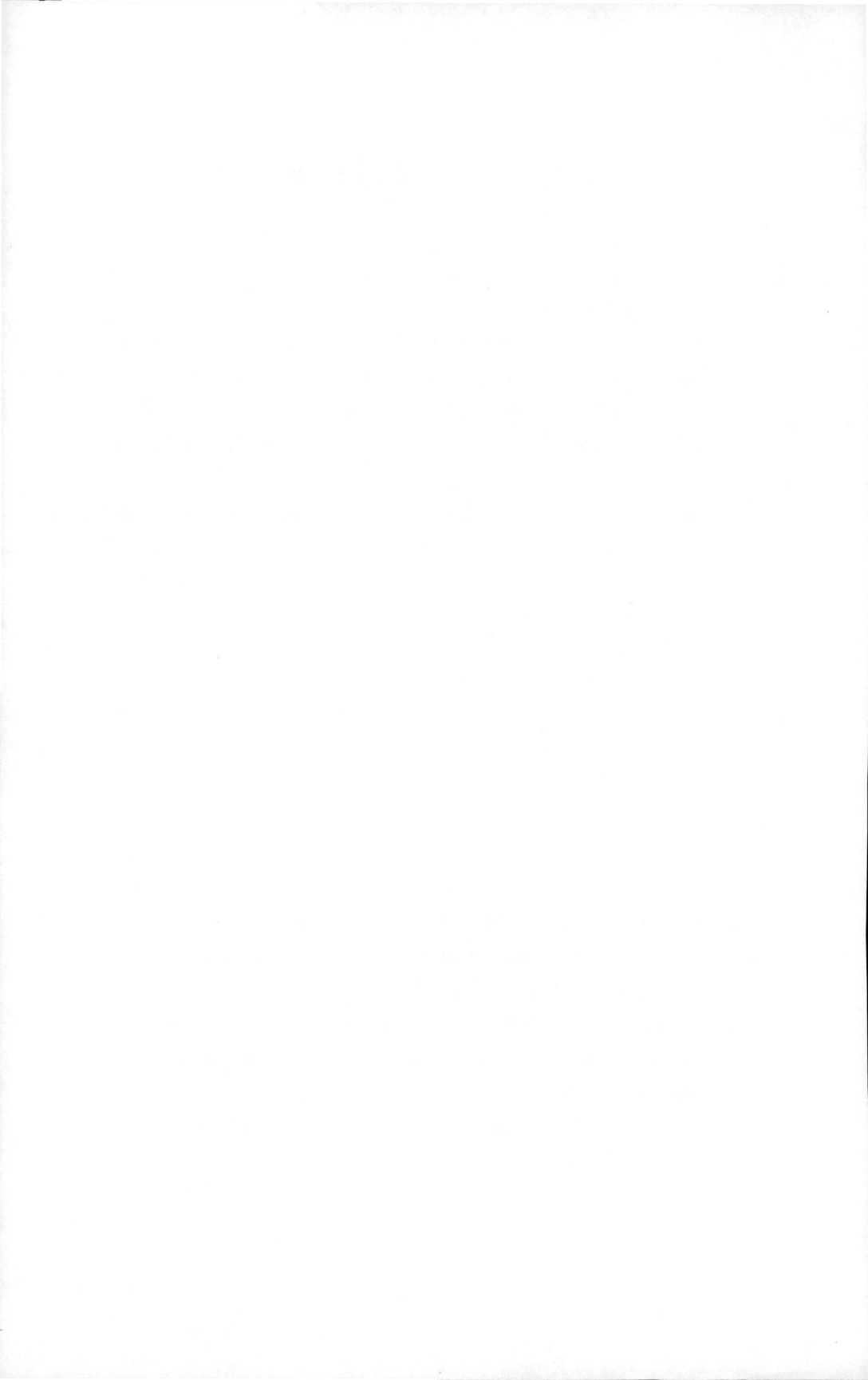

# Influencing
# TODAY'S
# YOUTH

## Shaping the Behaviors, Expectations, and Aspirations of Tomorrow's Leaders

### Danita Johnson Hughes, Ph.D.

Influencing Today's Youth
Shaping the Behaviors, Expectations, and Aspirations of Tomorrow's Leaders
by Danita Johnson Hughes, Ph.D.

ISBN: 978-0-615-60538-8

Library of Congress Control Number: 2012937799

Published by: Vitality Ventures, Inc.
909 Buckthorne Court, Valparaiso, IN 46383
United States of America

First Edition

Printed in the United States of America

To purchase additional copies of this book, please visit
www.danitajohnsonhughes.com

To our youth—may you be influenced to find your way
and light the path for generations to come.

# Contents

# Introduction

*"Your words and influence will plant the seed of either success or failure in the mind of another."*
~ Napoleon Hill

*"T*hings sure are different today compared to when I was a kid."

Have you ever heard yourself say these words? I've certainly said them, and I'm sure we all have at one point. That's because society and today's generation *are* different from when we were younger. However, different doesn't mean bad or good. It's just…well…different.

You don't have to look too hard to see the differences everywhere. From 100+ television stations on cable to information at your fingertips via the Internet, today's youth are being raised in an extraordinarily fast-paced, high-tech world…and the pace and speed of information will only increase as the years go by.

As a result, we see many traits in today's youth that are difficult for adults to understand, namely:

- Many children are too complacent and are willing to settle for mediocrity. After all, why write a report on a topic when all the information is already there online about it, or when you can find someone half a world away to write it for you?

- Today's youth seem unwilling to defer immediate gratification. Technology has created an "I want it now" culture. In the past, children wrote letters (even had pen pals), and they relied on landline telephones or face-to-face communication. Today's kids have cell phones, instant messaging, texting, Skype, in addition to the more traditional communication methods.

They get the answers they are seeking immediately and expect everything else to occur just as quickly.

- Too many children seem unwilling to risk failure. Our "instant" culture has resulted in kids wanting not only quick and positive results, but they also want it for little effort. As such, many seem unwilling to stick with an endeavor for the long-term.

But, here's the irony: As much as things have changed, they have also remained the same. The only difference is that the problems and challenges today occur at a different time and space. In other words, the external stimuli or factors that create the challenges are different (i.e. technological advances have created differences in the way kids learn, work, are socialized, etc.), but the questions surrounding kids and how we raise them are identical to the questions and challenges from generations ago, namely:

- How do we assure that our children receive a good education?

- How do we keep them safe?

- Who are their friends?

- How do we teach them to be civil in their interactions with others?

- How do we prepare them for future success?

- How do we influence them to be the best they can be?

## The Art of Influence

The key to overcoming so many of today's challenges with youth can be summed up in one word: *Influence.*

When you properly influence young people, you are able to shape their behaviors, expectations, and aspirations. You're able to encourage positive social, emotional, and intellectual development—what we all want for today's children.

The Merriam-Webster dictionary defines influence as "The act or power of producing an effect without apparent exertion of force or direct exercise of command; corrupt interference with authority for personal gain; the power or capacity of causing an effect in indirect or intangible ways."

Influence is definitely an important word in today's society. We influence others and are influenced by others on a daily basis. Influence comes from many sources: an advertisement on television promising you'll be slim in 60 days or less, a boss encouraging you to stretch your workplace skills, a schoolyard bully taunting another child, and even a sweet-faced toddler pouting to get another piece of candy.

Influence is everywhere.

It's hard enough for you, as an adult, to manage the influences in the world. Think about what it's like for a young person who is ill equipped to manage the flood of influence bombarding him or her every day.

Obviously, not all influence is negative. And that's where you come in—*to be a positive source of influence on the youth in your life, whether you're a parent, grandparent, aunt, uncle, teacher, coach, neighbor, or someone who works with or interacts with kids on a regular basis.* Additionally, parents, caregivers, and other concerned adults can help by teaching kids to develop their own influence, also known as their internal GPS. Influence is the component of your GPS that instructs your values and reminds you of basic principles, like "Be kind to others." Influence is the bridge that leads to today's youth becoming tomorrow's productive citizens.

## Influence versus Control

Realize that influencing a child does not mean exerting control over him or her. In fact, the more I work with parents and children, the more I realize that many of the challenges families face come down to a matter of control. The adult is attempting to control the youth rather than influence him. While control may work for young children, the older kids get, the less effective control is. Once the child becomes a teenager, it becomes a battle of wills that invariably leads to a lose-lose outcome.

While the parents' intent may be to provide security and safety for their children, a controlling parent stifles the sense of responsibility and maturity we wants kids to have. It prevents kids from developing an important life skill—that of making positive choices.

Of course, the solution isn't to turn over complete control to our children. There are obvious ramifications to this response. Children need the guidance and mentorship of an adult.

So what is the balance between control and choice?

*Influence.*

Reaching today's youth is not about telling them what to do, making them listen, or forcing them to respect you; it's about influencing them to want to be the best they can be. Realize that when you raise kids with strict control over their decisions and behavior, and then overnight expect them to be responsible adults when they come of legal age, you'll be disappointed. Influence isn't a one-time act. Rather, it's a long-term outlook and approach to interacting with youth. The good news is that no matter where you are in your parenting journey (or your relationship with the youth in your life), you can start influencing them today.

## Why Influence?

As president of Edgewater Systems for Balanced Living, a comprehensive mental health care services provider in Gary, Indiana, I often see the worst effects of breakdowns in families, communities, and society. I see what happens when children have few or no positive influences in their lives. A common lament I hear from parents of teenagers is, "I wish my son (or daughter) would just take responsibility for his/her actions."

My reply often is, "How have you influenced your child to act responsibly over the years?" Most people are unsure of how to answer.

The fact is that your words and actions (or lack of them) influence youth. Kids can't learn what they haven't already been given or what they haven't witnessed from the adults in their lives. So if you want your child to be responsible, trusting, loving, mature, kind (you fill in the blank with whatever adjective you like), you need to be the influencer of those traits.

Unfortunately, I find that many adults today are too protective of children. It's so bad that the media and some experts have dubbed these hovering, in-their-child's-faces parents/adults as "helicopter parents." (Note: the label applies to more than just parents.) These adults pay such close attention to the child's problems and experiences that they stifle the development of necessary life skills, like responsibility, decision making, emotional maturity, etc.

So while a helicopter parent/adult has good intentions, the constant hovering and protection offered do little to influence or bolster the child's ability to take responsibility for his/her actions or make decisions that reflect strong values.

No matter what trait or value you want kids to demonstrate, you must influence the child to display that particular trait. It won't just occur because you desire it. For example, if you want your child to show respect to others, you must influence him or her to be respectful.

You do that by demonstrating respect yourself. How many times have you spoken to your child with a tone of disrespect (veiled in parental authority)? I have. Sometimes our emotions get the best of us. We're allowed occasional missteps. But if your regular modus operandi is that of disrespect, then that's the behavior you're influencing to appear in your children. Similarly, if you want to influence your children to listen better, then you have to listen first. Influence is about planting the seeds, and then nurturing them and watching them grow.

The essence of influence is amazingly simple. Children, especially young children, learn through observation. Your words have value, but not as much value as your actions.

Kids need to see what it means to take responsibility, have respect, listen, be kind, etc. Every day children are being influenced on critical life skills by friends, other adults, and the media. Often the lessons being taught are in conflict. Here's an example: My friends want me to lie about where I'm going after school so I can hang out with them.

A young person who has received little positive influence from adults is ill equipped to make a positive choice in this situation, because he has never been allowed to make a choice without his parents hovering over him or some other adult trying to exert control. But a child who has received proper influence—who has witnessed responsible behavior, who was given responsibility, and who was allowed to make choices (even small ones) in the past—has learned the life skills he needs to make a positive choice.

Despite our best attempts to influence children to make smart, responsible decisions and be the best they can be, will kids still slip up? Will they lie to their parents so they can hang out with their friends? Definitely! They're human, just like the adults in their lives. Mistakes come with the territory. But a child who has received positive influence—one who witnessed and was taught foundational life skills like responsibility, respect, and listening—will overcome those mistakes and learn from them.

## Start from the Inside Out

This book is designed to help you become a source of positive influence on the youth in your life. You'll learn how to connect with and inspire today's kids in a way that promotes positive life skills, mature decision-making, and responsible behavior. This book will help you influence youth through today's tough challenges, from respecting others, adopting healthy life habits, and making smart decisions about sex to taking education seriously, saying no to bullying, and learning to rise above failure.

As you read and apply the information, be ready to implement three key principles to make it all work:

1. **Be present.** We live in challenging times that are filled with many distractions for you and your children. Despite the busyness of life, commit to being available for your children and to be a core influencer. This means being physically present, but also emotionally present to tend to their needs.

2. **Be open.** Communication is a serious problem between parents and their children, and often influence depends on communication. Remember, influence isn't about telling, shouting, lecturing, or closed mindedness. Commit to being open to your children.

3. **Be a role model.** Ultimately, to influence anyone, you have to walk the talk. It's common advice that is less commonly acted upon. Yet, your actions have greater influence than your words, so be sure they line up!

I admit that I often worry for the lost children, the ones who have so much potential but don't have a beacon to guide their path, or an anchor to grasp when the challenges of life try to push them down. Fortunately, by reading this book and applying the information, you're making sure the children in your life are no longer "lost."

Yes, we live in challenging times. And it's in these moments that children are most susceptible to influence, positive or negative. So as you read, consider what you want most from the children in your life… and then take the steps to influence them in that direction.

# Chapter One

# My First Experience with Positive Influence

*"Often, one person can influence a child to find something in
herself and grow up to her full potential. When I was a child,
one person showed me the power of positive influence and made
that difference for me. You can be that person for someone else."*
~ Danita Johnson Hughes

When I was six years old my family moved to a house on Polk Street,
in Gary, Indiana. Like many children from unhappy families, I hoped
the change would do us good. No such luck. We packed our problems
with us. Those problems looked even uglier set against the beautiful
backdrop of our new neighborhood. Some of the families on Polk
Street were fairly well off. We were not. Some owned their own homes.
We lived in the basement of someone else's house.

My parents slept in one room, and my five brothers and sisters and
I slept in the other. In some ways, living in tight quarters made my siblings and me closer, but it also increased the tension in our family—
not to mention the teasing we suffered from the neighborhood kids:

"You live in a basement? With the rats?"

"They probably keep 'em as pets."

"Nah, they eat 'em!" That was Wanda, the meanest girl in my
neighborhood.

But we weren't as ashamed of our living quarters as we were of the
fact that the neighbors knew our family secrets. They could hear the

sounds of our father hollering at our mother, sometimes punctuated by a slap, a scream, or a piece of furniture falling over. They could see the bruises on my mother's face and the fingerprints on her arms. They could see our homemade clothes. Instead of pitying us, they did what kids have done for centuries: ganged up on us and mocked us.

"You wore that raggedy ol' dress yesterday."

"Don't your mother ever buy you new shoes?"

"Nah, their Daddy doesn't make any money," Wanda said.

"Just ignore them," my sister Denise muttered, as she lowered her head, tightened her hand around my fingers, and kept walking. But I couldn't shut out their laughter. Sometimes they followed us and threw things. Once, a group of boys beat up my brother Brad on the playground. I became afraid to go to school. I thought about hiding in the bushes and ditching class, anything to avoid the bullying and the stares. But I kept going because of Mrs. Kaufman.

I remember that Mrs. Kaufman was the prettiest teacher at Douglas Elementary. Maybe she was, or maybe she just looks that way in my memory because of the way she always smiled at me, as if I were someone important. She was young, maybe in her mid-twenties. At the time I thought she was the smartest person I ever met, and it made me feel good to know that a young, pretty woman could be so smart. Most important, she seemed to really like me.

"That's a beautiful picture, Danita. You're so creative with colors!"

"Good penmanship, Danita. Keep it up."

And when I came in alone from the playground, looking dejected: "Don't you worry, Danita. A nice girl like you will make lots of friends. Sometimes it just takes a while. You wait and see."

One day she asked me if I'd like to stay after school and help her. After that, she let me stay every day, and she even asked me to help her grade papers. Around other children I felt so helpless, and around my parents I felt so worthless; I was excited to think that someone thought

I had anything to contribute in the way of "help." For the first time in my life someone was treating me like I was special. I thought, "I must be pretty smart for someone as smart as Mrs. Kaufman to let me help grade papers!"

A lot of kids would have hated staying after class. But I didn't mind. It was nicer than being taunted all the way home, and it was nicer than going back to my crowded home, where my brothers and sisters were always so noisy I could barely do my homework. It was nicer than being ignored by my overwrought mother, who was always busy doing housework or cooking dinner or arguing with my father.

"Why isn't dinner ready yet?"

"Don't pressure me. I worked hard all day!"

"And I didn't? Don't tell me about working hard!"

"There's no need to shout in front of the kids!"

"Don't tell me what to do!"

Mama didn't seem to notice when I stayed late after school. I suppose it was easier than having one more person to deal with.

But I didn't do it for my mother. I did it for me, and for Mrs. Kaufman. One day early on Mrs. Kaufman told me, "You're such a big help to me. You deserve to be paid for your hard work. So I'm going to give you a dime every time you stay and help."

"You don't have to pay me, Mrs. Kaufman."

"I insist. When people do excellent schoolwork, they receive an 'A' as their reward. When people do work for others, they receive payment. You keep that money. You earned it."

I grinned from ear to ear.

I still remember the bright shine and sharp metallic smell of those dimes—one for each afternoon. My first wages! I was so proud. Those dimes represented a new world to me. They represented independence. I could buy candy at the local five-and-dime without having to ask my parents for spare change I knew they didn't have.

I didn't realize it then, but looking back I understand that Mrs. Kaufman could see how lonely I was. I wasn't the only child in her class to get picked on. But I was probably the poorest. The faded dresses hinted at it. The shoes gave it away.

My shoes weren't just worn out; they were ragged. At any given time, I only owned one pair. I always wore each pair until long after larges holes gaped in the bottoms. I can remember many mornings putting cardboard in my shoes to keep my socks from getting dirty. I can remember coming home at the end of each day, taking off my only pair of socks, and washing them out in the sink so I could wear them again the next day. Mrs. Kaufman must have noticed the state of my shoes, but she never said a word about them.

One afternoon, after the final bell rang and the other students left, I walked up to her desk as I always did to ask if I could help with anything.

"Yes, as a matter of fact, you can," she said. She opened her bottom drawer and pulled out a pair of brand new shoes. They were shiny black patent leather, prettier than any shoes I'd ever owned. I stared at them longingly, and then looked up at her shyly as she explained, "I bought these for my niece, but they're too small for her. They were on sale, so the store won't take them back. I don't know what else to do with them, and I thought you might as well have them."

"Really?"

"Unless you don't like them. Then, I guess I'll just have to throw them out."

"No, don't throw them away. I like them very much. Thank you, Mrs. Kaufman."

I was so excited to wear them the next day. I didn't even care that the shiny shoes made my handmade dress appear even shabbier. No one would make fun of my shoes today. They were brand spanking new. Even Wanda didn't own a pair as pretty. Although I may have been a little embarrassed about accepting them, Mrs. Kaufman never treated me like I needed charity. She made it clear that I was a big help to her, and that she was just helping me out in return. Her niece couldn't use the shoes, so why not pass them along to me?

Mrs. Kaufman gave me a lot more than a few shiny dimes or a pair of shoes. Mrs. Kaufman taught me the value of work, and the joy of helping others. She gave me a safe haven in a comfortable place after school. She gave me a role model. From her I received love and understanding and a feeling of my own worth. That was a gift I would later become eager to pass on to others.

Thank you, Mrs. Kaufman.

Why do I tell you this story?

Mrs. Kaufman was the first adult who was a positive influence in my life. Her gift of influence showed me that I was special. And because of the difference Mrs. Kaufman made in my life, I didn't give up on myself. My family remained poor, and I remained lonely throughout my childhood. But I kept going to school. In my search for love, I had sex too young, got pregnant, and had to drop out of high school to become a working mother. But I promised myself I would go back to school. Thanks to the belief in myself that Mrs. Kaufman helped inspire, I didn't give up. I *did* go back to school. Not only did I finish high school, I eventually earned a bachelor's degree, two master's degrees, and a Ph.D.

Mrs. Kaufman wasn't the only person who influenced me to be the best I could be. But she was the first, and if it hadn't been for her, I might not have been so ready to listen to and learn from the others who came along.

Mrs. Kaufman made possible my own individual story of achieving more than the statistics said I would. Let's face it: the outlook for a teenage mother and high school dropout from a background of poverty and domestic violence is not usually a good one. The stereotypes suggested a different outcome for my life. But Mrs. Kaufman, and the people who influenced me after her, made me believe I could become something more than a stereotype.

Mrs. Kaufman helped me because she knew that individuals matter—and only individuals matter. If we look at the people of our country as a series of demographics and statistics—numbers and characteristics organized in categorized and stereotyped groups—we will lose sight of that important truth. Worse than that, we will lose our children. After all, you don't influence numbers—you influence people.

You can take a step toward helping to positively influence the children in your life by learning to do what Mrs. Kaufman did: commit to shaping the behaviors, expectations, and aspirations of the young people you interact with.

Whether you're dealing with a young family member (child, niece, nephew, grandchild, stepchild, etc.) or a child in your community, school, or practice, extend yourself just a little bit more. Offer some words, some actions, or some other way to help that young person discover her potential, and show her the skills she'll need to achieve that potential. Then trust that your influence and example will inspire other adults to do the same. Trust that your actions will inspire that child to pass on the favor when she is ready. And trust that the joy you receive from being a positive influence will reward you—and will energize you to extend yourself to the next child you encounter as well.

This is how we can set the wheels in motion to influence a hundred, a thousand, a million children.

Our responsibility to children doesn't begin and end with parenting. It starts with the idea that we are all part of a community, and that we influence those around us, whether we intend to or not. So why not use your intention to influence others in a positive way.

You can help a child see a bigger future, as Mrs. Kaufman did for me. And no, it's not always about giving children a gift, a job, or a safe haven. Being an influence occurs in both small and large gestures. Here are some other examples of what influence can look like:

- Making it a point to smile and say hello to the children you pass by in your neighborhood rather than simply hurry by.

- Acknowledging a child's accomplishments, no matter how small: "You tried really hard on that test—good effort." "That was wonderful how you helped Mr. Smith with his groceries." "You're a great (football player, singer, artist, etc.)."

- Allowing a child to dream with you. For example, "What would you love your future to look like?" Then let the child talk without interruptions and without "reality" thinking, as in, "Yes, but you need a lot of education or money to do that."

- Setting the bar high by exemplifying the behavior you desire. Remember, influence comes from what you do as much as from what you say.

- Getting involved with a formal organization, such as the Boys and Girls Club, or any other charitable organization that caters to children's needs in your area. Many organizations work to help children in need. They're almost always under-funded and understaffed, and they're typically thrilled to find dedicated volunteers who want to influence a child.

- Developing a close connection with your children. Children who are close to their parents tend to be more grounded and secure in who they are, which enables them to be strong when negative influences come their way.

- Encouraging individuality. Everyone, adult or child, wants to fit in. Those who don't have a healthy balance between acceptance and independence often suffer from negative influences. Teach your children the importance of being their own person and always doing what's right for them.

- Supporting positive influencers. Be aware of who your children interact with, even from a very early age. Teach them to seek out positive qualities in their friends and also model what it means to be a positive influence on others (sometimes it's your kid who is the negative influence!).

- Listening to the children in your life. Listening helps you to understand them. The more you understand them, the more you will be able to influence them.

- Introducing them to people who make good role models. It is easier to make an impression on kids the younger they are. As they get older, they learn to emulate positive behaviors that they have been exposed to.

- Encouraging the children in your life to follow through on their interests. Introduce them to people, places, and activities that support their interests. Be slow to criticize or judge, as this could dampen their enthusiasm.

You don't need to be a childhood education expert, social worker, or psychologist to do any of these things. You only need to take an interest in the children you interact with. Often, all a child needs to help her reach her potential is someone to talk to and ask questions of, someone who cares about her setbacks and accomplishments, someone who shows a genuine interest in her.

As adults we face important issues: spirituality, success, failure, crime, education, sexuality, health, and parenting. Our ability to deal with these issues from a place of strength begins with a strong foundation in childhood. It's easier for people to become self-confident adults prepared to achieve personal success and create strong communities if someone first teaches confidence to those people when they are young. Self-confidence is a gift that adults give themselves, but it doesn't start that way. It begins as a gift we receive from adults when we are children. Not all parents are functionally equipped to provide that gift. That's where you can be the influence who helps.

In the following chapters, I'm going to tell you stories about real people who have influenced and been influenced, and share strategies you can use with the youth in your life so they can go on to reach their full potential. I'm not asking you to become like the people you find in this book. I'm asking you to find your unique strengths and apply them to your life and interactions today. So I invite you to use this book as a starting point for your own thought and discussion. Look within yourself and envision how you can help us all shoulder the great responsibility we have to raise our children well. Help the keepers of your community's future find their path, and if they stray from that path, influence them to redirect so they can embrace a successful and prosperous future.

# Chapter Two

# It's Everyone's Responsibility to Influence the Future

*"You can never really live anyone else's life, not even your child's.
The influence you exert is through your own life,
and what you've become yourself."*
~ Eleanor Roosevelt

The more you influence today's children, the more you'll contribute to transforming the world. Taking the first steps of that influence and transformation journey begins when we work to change the circumstances in our immediate sphere of influence. We begin to impact our circumstances more powerfully when we connect with other people. We connect with others more profoundly when we understand our true selves. We cannot do any of these things, until we begin to take *responsibility*. Taking responsibility to influence today's youth begins with taking responsibility for ourselves and our part in the world. Whatever change you seek to create in your nation, your community, your home, or yourself, you must, at some point, be willing to let the buck stop with you.

While anyone can unknowingly influence someone either positively or negatively, what I'm referring to is making the conscious decision to be a positive influence in people's lives. That kind of commitment requires responsibility.

I believe responsibility takes place on three levels. Let's call these levels: personal, proximal, and social.

## Three Levels of Responsibility

1) **Personal:** Personal responsibility requires introspection. To take responsibility for yourself, your actions, and your life's results, you must first know who you are and what you value. When you take responsibility, you create worthy goals that will help you become your best self and benefit others. When you take responsibility, you get the information and develop the relationships you need to pursue those goals. When you take responsibility, you take action on those goals without waiting for others to do that for you.

   Taking responsibility doesn't mean that you will accept the label of a good or bad person based on your results. It means that you will be accountable for doing your best to obtain good results and turn those results to your advantage, or that you will be accountable for cleaning up bad results and trying to turn them around. If you succeed, you accept the rewards. If you fail, you accept the consequences. Responsibility means neither blaming others for your mistakes, nor blaming yourself. When you fail, you acknowledge your failure. You assess what you did right, what you did wrong, and then move on to create new goals.

   People who take responsibility are open to new ideas, open to other people, open to the world and their part in it. Responsible people do not live in fear of failure or in expectation of success, but simply understand that results require work. They accept both life's rewards and its difficulties with grace.

2) **Proximal:** Proximal responsibility refers to taking responsibility to support our family members, friends, neighbors, and colleagues, by giving them honest feedback, sharing

information, encouraging them when their actions positively impact us or our community, and holding them accountable when that impact is negative.

When reaching out to others seems like too much work, or feels embarrassing or intrusive, it's tempting to beg off with the excuse that you're not your "brother's keeper." True, you're not personally responsible for what other people do or what happens to them—unless you do something to directly help, hurt, or hinder them. Yet, people cannot survive or thrive without mutual support. If you don't reach out to help keep your fellow human from stumbling, or if you have the power to help someone with potential rise to meet that potential and you fail to do so, then you'll have a much smaller support system to rely on in your own efforts to sustain and improve your life. When you reach out to your fellows, you add another link in the strong chain needed to build the kind of community that benefits us all.

3) **Social:** Social responsibility is built on interlocking relationships in which we all take responsibility for each other as a group. Someone who takes action to make a difference in his community, country, or world, understands that the change he effects will ultimately trickle back down to individuals, to one person. He knows that can mean himself or his sister, father, daughter, or friend. He knows that by reaching out to impact the greater good, he strengthens the bonds that tie us all together on this planet, increasing all of our chances to survive and thrive and live in peace.

Social responsibility means taking a look at the issues that affect you as an individual and, instead of complaining or assigning blame, asking what you can do to influence that issue

for everyone. People who take social responsibility understand that it really is "a small world, after all," that everything
we do or fail to do affects everyone else, and vice versa. When
we contribute positive things into that larger system, we
make life easier for others, making it more likely they'll also
contribute positive things, making it more likely for all our
lives to improve. When we gripe and complain from the
sidelines, or worse, throw more problems into the mix—
like giving in to the urge to hit our children, being mean or
uncaring toward someone, or allowing gossip to spread—
we make the world a little worse for all of us.

## An Integrated Approach

It's tempting to look at these three levels of responsibility as separate.
It's tempting to think that if you're on top of one of these levels,
you've got it covered. Certainly, personal responsibility can be a strong
foundation for the other two. Definitely, even the most profoundly
world-changing journey begins with a single step. However, I would
venture this: if you truly want to influence today's youth, your goal
should be to ultimately attain all three levels in your life, because none
of the three levels of responsibility works as well without the others.
In the strongest individuals, relationships, and organizations, each level
provides support and strength for the other two.

It's true that if everyone took personal responsibility we would have
less need for people to take on social responsibility. If all of us each
kept our little corner of the world clean and swept up, then no one
would ever have to take responsibility for anyone else. But how long
do you think you'll sit around waiting for *everyone* to get on the ball
with that one? How far has that kind of thinking gone to changing your
community so far? And by the way, just how big is your corner of the
world, anyway, before it starts to intrude on someone else's corner?

The simple fact is, when the stronger among us take *social* responsibility, we make it easier for those weaker than ourselves to take *personal* responsibility. Maybe you don't think you're one of those stronger people, or you don't want to be. Sorry: you are. If you weren't, you probably wouldn't have picked up this book. Maybe you don't think it's fair that people are always relying on you. Perhaps, but neither is it fair that some people are born without the strength you have.

If you have the talent and strength to take social responsibility to help influence the future generation of your community, then you have the responsibility to use that talent and strength to do so. Actually, if you consider it from the point of view of Luke, you'll see that this extra requirement given to us stronger types is actually quite fair: *"For everyone to whom much is given, from him much will be required; and to whom much has been committed, of him they will ask the more." Luke 12:48*

And about everyone cleaning up his or her corner: the truth is our little corner always affects someone else's little corner. When we clean up the dust over here, it often settles on someone else's porch. When you buy more consumer goods, you help create jobs; when you buy more consumer goods, you also help increase factory pollution. What's it going to be? Can we create more jobs without creating pollution? Probably. But only if you acknowledge that the stuff in your corner is no longer just in your corner.

So individual responsibility becomes social responsibility, and social responsibility becomes individual responsibility. Meanwhile, proximal responsibility becomes the glue that holds it all together.

It's easier for groups and individuals to relate to each other, for social responsibility to meet individual responsibility, when we connect to it all through the lens of one-to-one relationships. When we're accountable to each other and for each other, we strengthen our identities as individuals while also strengthening our ties to the group.

At some point, we must all face the consequences of our choices alone. No one can do it for us. At some point, others will also face the consequences of our choices. We live in a world with other people; it's inevitable our choices will affect them. Every failure of government, every financial debacle in the business world, every rift in our families, can typically be traced back to someone's failure to take responsibility for his or her part in a problem, or its solution.

Our nation's education system is falling behind, in part because some lawmakers and taxpayers don't want to pay the true cost of quality education, in part because some teachers don't want to be held accountable for results, in part because some parents won't do what it takes to give children the security and support necessary for effective learning, and in part because many of today's children are growing up with either a sense of futility or a sense of entitlement—none of which reflects an attitude of responsibility.

Taking responsibility for my life and my actions is the foundation I established before I began taking on the proximal responsibility of helping other individuals, which then taught me the skills I needed to take on greater social responsibility. To some extent, I think this path should be everyone's goal. Don't be afraid if this seems like too much. Perhaps for now the biggest way you feel you can influence someone is to simply smile and show kindness. That's okay. Start small if you need to. Over time, little influences add up.

In my own family history I've seen the seeds of negativity, and the resulting crop of failure that comes from an unwillingness to take responsibility. Although I later found help along the way, there was only one person who could take the first step to turn away from that history, toward a brighter future: me.

## The Roots of Responsibility

I wasn't responsible for being born into a background of poverty, and I wasn't responsible for my upbringing in a household full of abuse, neglect, and negative influence. However, I was responsible for overcoming those setbacks, as well as the obstacles I created for myself because I resented the cards life had dealt me. As an adult, it was up to me to make my life what I wanted it to be.

At the beginning, I did waste some time blaming others for my problems and failures. As a young single mother cleaning bedpans at a mental hospital, I walked around with a huge, angry chip on my shoulder. Maybe I had good reasons to be angry, but my reasons, good or bad, were irrelevant—my constant, unremitting anger was counterproductive. It only made things worse, not better.

If I was going to create the life I wanted, I had to take responsibility for it. I knew I needed to take action, but I didn't know which direction to go. So I needed to get other people on board to help me with advice and information. I couldn't do that unless I developed a willingness to ask for and receive help, as well as a willingness to give something in return. So my first step was internal: I had to create a more positive outlook.

This was not easy. At first I had few role models or mentors to go by.

When I was growing up, my parents didn't provide the best role models for a strong code of personal or proximal responsibility, not to mention social responsibility—an idea completely outside their realm of thinking. In terms of personal responsibility, my father always blamed rotten luck for his lot in life, and my mother, who was trapped in the social norms of the day, was totally dependent on my father, putting him in charge of her life.

My mother left my father multiple times. He was not a responsible husband or father, and leaving him was the right idea. However, probably because she didn't know what to say about the situation to us kids, she never explained what she was doing, what was going to happen to us as a result, or why. Looking back, she was really just another victim of the times—when women had few resources to help them leave an abusive relationship.

Left to his own irresponsible devices, my father took out his frustration with their relationship on us children. One of the defining moments of my dysfunctional relationship with my dad came the day he gathered the six older kids together and told us that my mother had left him and they were likely to get a divorce. He said, "I want you guys to tell me who you want to live with, and you can tell me the truth." My brothers were old enough to sense the need for diplomacy and claimed that they wanted to live with both parents. But I was a small child who wanted to trust my father. Since he told us he wanted the truth, I took his word for it and said, "I want to live with my mother." He called me stupid, and I felt betrayed. Talk about a negative influence!

My father had told me to be honest, but he didn't really want me to be honest. That was my first lesson in responsibility, or rather, irresponsibility. Dad failed to do his duty as a parent: to give his children a sense of self-worth and security, and to teach us the social skills that would prepare us for happy, productive lives. His communication skills are certainly not what I use today to obtain results from my employees and clients, much less my own family.

But that was just the worst of my father's many irresponsible betrayals of his wife and children. I remember one day Dad was getting ready to leave for work, and my Mom and three of us kids were following him toward the door. He was at top of the stairs. We kids were playing on the stairway, and the youngest fell off. Dad turned and accused me of deliberately pushing my sister off the stairs and insisted that my mother should whip me.

My mother said, "No, she didn't push her." But Dad insisted that he saw it and she'd better hit me. She was used to following his orders—she had no choice. So after he left, she whipped me, even though he wasn't there to see anymore, and even though she didn't believe I'd done anything wrong. In her knee-jerk habit of protecting herself, she failed to protect her children. In the end, she didn't protect herself, either: she stayed with a violent, emotionally cruel, unfaithful man.

Dad beat my mother up often enough that it wasn't uncommon to see her with a black eye. We never had friends over because our dad made it clear in no uncertain terms that he didn't want other kids running around his house, even when he wasn't there. As we grew older, all of us kids used to beg Mom, "You need to leave him." She said she couldn't leave because she loved him and because she couldn't support all of us, or even just herself, on her own. This was partly true: it was hard in those days for women to find work. She sometimes did domestic work, but she was a stay-at-home mom for most of our lives.

Our mother felt economically trapped.

Even now I believe that some part of that was an excuse, a forgivable, understandable excuse, from a woman trapped by the times and her circumstances—yet, in the end, it was still an excuse. I often saw other kids down the street who lived with single moms and, even though they were poorer than we were, they seemed healthier, without the jumpy anxiety of the kids in our family. Their mothers weren't cowering, frightened women with shiners on their eyes. Those families didn't have a lot, but they made their lives work, and they were happier because their lives were free of abuse. But my mother let fear overcome reason.

I know my mother wanted a better life for all of us. But she was another victim, like us. Dad threatened her constantly, and when she did leave he often went looking for her. I understand why she was scared, possibly for her very life. Such acts of private domestic terrorism were his responsibility, not hers.

It was my father who failed the most spectacularly at proximal responsibility. He rarely came home. He made auto parts, and he worked long hours all week and came home tired. Then every Friday, he would come home, get showered and dressed up, and spend the entire weekend away from home. He wouldn't come back until Monday morning. My mother got up early every Monday, fed him breakfast, made him lunch, and sent him off to work. She rarely said a word about him being gone every weekend. She clearly felt helpless to do anything about it.

Since he was such an irresponsible parent all around, it was a backhanded blessing that he wasn't home more often. We kids liked it when he was gone, because things were calmer and more fun and friendly at those times. We enjoyed our mother more when he wasn't there. But that's because he was a tyrant. If he had been a good father, it would have been better to have him home. The fact that we didn't have a father at home created a definite hole in our lives. Had he made an effort to be there to guide us—to influence us—when we had difficulties, it might have helped.

My father's one-two punch of absence and abuse was the biggest abdication of responsibility I witnessed in my young life.

I learned at a young age the reason my father was away so much. When my younger sister was one or two years old, my dad took her out with him frequently when he left the house for long stretches of time. He'd have my mom dress her up and then he'd take her with him. I was maybe about four or five, and I was jealous that he would take my sister out and not me. One day I whined that I wanted to go, too, and he decided to take me.

I remember he took me to this woman's house, and I remember she gave me a small bed for my doll. At the time, I didn't understand who she was. Dad told me she was his "pen pal." I told my mom that dad took me to meet his "pen pal." She was obviously hurt and told me not to tell her that. That's when I began to understand that my dad was doing something wrong with these other women—he was "cheating" on my mother.

In almost every way, my father failed to present a proper role model. He often lectured us about what to do and not to do, but as the old saying goes, "He didn't practice what he preached." In retrospect, if he were going to be unfaithful, it would have been better if he'd done more to hide that fact from his children. We didn't need to know about his shortcomings. It was incumbent on him to present a more favorable model and a better influence on his own children.

The things he did directly in our presence were even worse. He talked down to my mother and belittled her in public, around friends, family, anyone. Sometimes he called her stupid, or told her she was embarrassing him, or teased her about her appearance. People would stare at all of us. We could see the hurt on her face, but she silently accepted his put-downs. He should have shown restraint, not only for her and for us—he should have respected himself more. I now know he grew up in a house that enabled his irresponsibility. Abuse of power was passed on from generation to generation, by example.

A responsible father would have shown us how to respect other people, by respecting our mother. Instead, he browbeat her so much that she felt devalued as a human being. As a result, her self-respect suffered. Had she felt more self-confident, she could have shown us how to respect ourselves by asserting herself as an individual and insisting on respect from her husband. Instead, she let my father's cruelty define her. They both should have let us know we were valuable and loved, by giving us a safe environment in which to grow up. Instead, our parents taught us that relationships were all about cruel offense and terrified defense.

Without better examples, we grew up unsure of how to behave in relationships. One of my sisters ended up in an abusive relationship. Early on I had abusive boyfriends, too. However, over time I recognized that I had to take responsibility for my own life. I couldn't blame my parents for my adult life choices. I had the choice to change. So I did.

Here's where other people's failure to take social responsibility comes into the picture. The way women were devalued by society in my mother's day didn't help, and indeed hindered her from getting the support she needed to make it more feasible for her to leave my father. She didn't have a skill set that would have allowed her to enter the work force and earn a livable wage because she didn't graduate from high school. He didn't graduate either, but as a man he could get a good-paying job in a factory. Women didn't have that kind of option. Maybe if she'd had that option she would have felt more able to take the risk of asserting her independence.

Another failure on the social responsibility front: in those days, society gave unspoken yet tacit acceptance of men beating up their wives. There weren't strong laws protecting women from abuse. So society taught my mother that her role should rightly be that of a victim without a voice. Meanwhile society taught my father that he was the head of the household; therefore, his role was that of breadwinner, and his word and fist were law in his house.

My dad saw it that way until he passed away. He even encouraged his daughters' husbands to "put their wives in their place." When one of my sisters got into an argument with her husband and my Dad over-heard, he told her husband, "A woman needs her ass whipped every now and then." Her husband was dumbfounded. My brother-in-law later told my sister how appalled he was at my father's medieval attitude. He said, "How could a man ever tell another man to hit his daughter?" My brother-in-law's reaction shows that social attitudes are subject to influence just as much as children are.

So, too, my success as a woman leader is proof that a person's willingness to take personal responsibility can trump the drawbacks of a past full of parental irresponsibility. A little luck helps, but we must be willing to take advantage of our luck. Through the years I did have people in my life, or sought out people, who saw my potential and helped nurture that little seed.

My paternal grandmother was a big influence. She was not huggy, kissy, or demonstrative; she was strict, and didn't show a lot of affection. Yet she was someone I could talk to, and she always saw my father's flaws. She recognized her son's abusiveness, his affairs, his cruelty to his own children, and she made it clear she disapproved. By doing that, she let me know that his behavior was wrong, and I allowed myself to learn that lesson. She let me unload on her when things got rough, and she affirmed my feelings. My grandmother was brutally honest, so I felt always that I had a trustworthy ally in her. Grandma said, "Don't marry someone who ever hits you or says mean things to you." I took her words to heart.

Over the years I sought other people who gave me solid advice that rang as true as my grandmother's. It just goes to show how much you can grow from the smallest seeds that other people plant in your life. So, no matter how difficult your past, there's always something there you can use as a foundation to build upon. There's rarely any excuse to wallow in self-pity. We all have these seeds of possibility in our lives, and we have the choice to seek water and fertilizer for those seeds and help them grow, or to focus on the bad and let our potential wither away.

Taking personal responsibility is easier if you seek other people who've demonstrated an affinity for proximal responsibility, people who've shown the talent and willingness to influence other people's lives. Ask such people for support. Having a support system that's readily available to you is important. If one hasn't come your way, then go out and find one. Create that support system for yourself. Invite people into your life who make you feel like you're worth something. Send other people on their way. It's important to remember that it's an honor and a privilege for others to be invited into your inner circle. Reserve that space for those who genuinely have your best interests at heart.

That doesn't mean you shouldn't keep people around who sometimes tell you difficult truths about yourself. When someone offers criticism, take a moment to think about where they're coming from. If it's clear they're trying to be of service, and that you may benefit from making a change they suggest, you might not want to be too quick to blame them for "negativity" and push them out of your life. This is why it's good to have more than one person of influence in your life. Sometimes you need an outside perspective to begin to see whether someone is offering you helpful advice, or simply dumping on you. Dump the dumpers, keep the honest supporters.

To overcome adversity, you have to have a strong belief in yourself. But you can create that belief starting with very little. It just takes a lot of hard work to build on that. Develop a mindset that you can make it, and that you want to make it. I grew determined that I wasn't going to fail like my father expected me to. A good part of my success came from my desire to fight: I wasn't going to let my dad or anyone else define me.

You might start with little more than the knowledge that you want something more. That's okay. At first it's just important to pick something, anything, positive to move toward. That's what I did. Once you get started, then you need to commit yourself to refine and clarify what it is you want to accomplish and become. Your aspirations may change over time; they may change several times. Mine did. If you're already moving in a positive direction, it's easier to change gears. That's what I've discovered.

Wrap your mind around something positive you can do for a young person in your life, whether it's offering encouragement to a struggling teen or embarking in a formal mentorship program. Once you've identified something, take some action to make it happen—any action. This is how we influence others: one step at a time.

You have to persevere, because at times you may fall back to old behaviors. People, circumstances, or other factors make it difficult to always be a positive influence. Sometimes people throw roadblocks up, intentionally or not. You must not let obstacles or challenges stop you, but maneuver through them all and stay on course. Just keep moving, even if you only make progress by fits and starts.

To help you stay motivated as you embark on this new mindset and commitment to be an influence to others, make it a point to celebrate small successes along the way. Look at small things you can influence others to achieve, and let success at those small things push your vision to grow.

## Pay It Forward

Throughout my life, people have influenced me in a way that has truly made a difference in my success. In turn, in my career today, I regularly strive to influence children and adults with social, behavioral, and mental problems—people who need plenty of support just to survive, much less thrive and find their own way to success. In all my dealings with people from all walks of life, I see one constant: everybody needs positive influences in their lives. After all the support I've had turning my life around, it only feels natural to do anything I can to help other people change their own lives.

It's very rewarding to influence and contribute to an individual or a group that truly wants and needs what you can offer, and to then watch your guidance and help make a difference. I've always enjoyed challenges. That's why I joined Edgewater Systems for Balanced Living back when it was a mental health organization in trouble. I helped them get back on course: partly by applying a system with a clearer plan and more accountability, partly by creating a stronger support system for our organization, both internal and external.

It's deeply rewarding to see and feel our clients and employees benefit from the changes that I helped influence and create. To see how these positive changes affect not only individuals, but also our entire community, helps me to see the power each of us has when we work together. I feel that I'm giving something back, with a lot of help from others.

I wouldn't be here if someone hadn't been there to influence, encourage, and assist me, back when I needed help. Today I take social responsibility on a larger scale, because I now have the skills and the network to do so. I know if I don't step forward, somebody else might not. Not everyone is ready for leadership. I am. I have been given much, so I believe much is required of me.

I owe it not just to myself, but to those around me, not to just breathe the air. All of us, every last one of us who has attained anything of value in this world, have been helped and influenced by someone along the way. If we don't pass that along, that unexpected helping hand might not be there for us again in the future. It's our responsibility to improve our community, our homes, and our world. It won't happen without all of us pulling together. To the extent we can, we have to be responsible for influencing the next generation. If not us, who?

Helping others helps the world as a whole in ways we can't measure. I'll give you an example:

Donnie was an eight-year-old boy who lived with his parents and five siblings. His father worked long hours frequently late into the night. His mother was the primary caretaker for the kids.

As the oldest child in the family, Donnie missed having his dad around to talk to and hang out with. Fortunately his Uncle Reggie, his mom's brother, visited regularly. Donnie enjoyed his company. Uncle Reggie played the guitar in a local band. He would practice on his guitar when he visited. He also took Donnie with him to rehearsals.

One day Uncle Reggie asked Donnie if he wanted to come with him to a wedding where he and the band would be playing. Donnie eagerly agreed to come along. He was so impressed with the performance and the crowd's reaction to the band that he decided then and there that he wanted to play in a band.

Uncle Reggie gave Donnie an old guitar to keep him encouraged. And although Donnie's parents could not afford to pay for guitar lessons, Donnie vowed that he was going to learn how to play on his own.

Uncle Reggie eventually got married and moved out of town. Donnie was devastated. But he was determined to continue practicing on his own. He practiced regularly and got better and better. Although he had not taken formal music lessons, he learned to play by ear.

As he got older, he and some of his friends formed a band. In high school they entered several talent contests and won in many of them. After graduation, the band continued to play. They now play regularly across the country for all kinds of celebrations and have become well known as entertainers.

Thanks to Uncle Reggie's early influence, Donnie is now an accomplished guitar player and is doing quite well at it. He is doing something he loves for a living and is contributing his talents to the world.

## Influence the Future

Now that you know about the three levels of responsibility and understand how they all work together, I hope you're eager to help influence today's youth. Of course, the next logical question is, "In what ways can my influence make the most impact?" That's what the remaining chapters will cover.

Remember, even the smallest positive act, word, or deed can influence a young person during a critical juncture. Believe that you have that power and your influence can help change the world.

# Chapter Three

# Influence Youth to
# Embrace a Sense of Family

*"Feelings of worth can flourish only in an atmosphere where
individual differences are appreciated, mistakes are tolerated,
communication is open, and rules are flexible—the kind of
atmosphere that is found in a nurturing family."*
~ Virginia Satir

In our complex world, loving families are a critical support system to help children reach their potential. When a child's family isn't supportive and doesn't provide the proper influence, that child can only succeed by creating alternative support systems. Somehow, children in these situations need to establish networks of people who keep them grounded and give them the influence their families aren't equipped to do.

This is where other concerned adults, like you, can step in. Yes, in the best possible world, all parents would offer their children a supportive environment and lots of positive influence that allows them to grow into their best possible selves. Parents would not only guide their children in proper ways of dealing with the world, but also encourage them to explore their own path. To fill our society with successful adults, we must provide children with both the discipline to stay on the path to success and the freedom to define success on their own terms.

Unfortunately, many children miss out on the second half of that equation. Their parents don't want them to succeed, don't care if they succeed, or don't have skills themselves to help and influence their children to do better. And when children miss out on this essential aspect of growing up, they tend to lack knowing what a true sense of family really is.

The good news is that any adult can influence children to embrace a sense of family. It's something that transcends biological lineage. How is this possible? Because having a sense of family is about connectedness, identification of respected values, and trust. All children and adolescents search for a sense of family (connectedness), and it's something that can be provided by adult role models. Ideally that role model will be a parent, but any adult can influence a child to embrace the values of taking care of self and others, honesty, respect, loyalty, and the unity of a group—in other words, a sense of family.

Realize that rather than live as isolated individuals, alone and void of any relationships, youth connect to some group—good or bad, young (like them) or adults. It is our inherent nature to fulfill a sense of family, and when the one that should be provided is not, the child will seek out another. Ultimately, almost all youth find some small group to connect to, whether it is family or an outside group.

Unfortunately, many of the "outside" choices available for the child to connect to are negative—for the child and the community. Ironically many of these groups, such as gangs, will teach the same values that are important for a family, but the values will be geared only toward the group's goals. In other words, the child will be taught loyalty—but only to the group—which will be contrary to the community's best interests. The most damaging thing is that these groups will teach the child to not trust others and to not aspire to achieve things outside of the group. But for the child, the only way to survive and have a connection is to join with the values and behaviors of the group.

However, when you become involved with youth and spend time building a positive relationship with them and the community in which they live, you are influencing a child to have a positive sense of family. Because of this relationship, the child will feel empowered and will value himself or herself as important. Once children start to believe in themselves, then they can be influenced to think of options and choices in their future that will make them successful.

## Influence in Action

At this point, people often wonder if an adult who has no biological relation to a child can really help that child embrace a sense of family. To that I offer the example of Brandon Freeland, a single young man who has never been married and who has taken on the responsibility of being a surrogate father to two boys, John and Kevin, due to their respective family circumstances. I know Brandon through my work at Edgewater Systems, and he is a true example of someone who has taken on proximal responsibility to positively influence two children who were desperately in need of guidance. Here are their stories.

## *John*

When John was 14, he started living with Brandon. John had a history of arrests and juvenile delinquency, and was very well known to the local court system and law enforcement. John had an older sister and brother, two nieces, and a nephew. These family members plus John's mother lived together in public housing and rented houses, usually with shady landlords. The family dynamics were very strained, and John was often viewed as a misfit and thief. As a result, John had little sense of family. In fact, he believed his biological family didn't care about him and felt he had to fend for himself. By the time he was 14, John was committing robberies and selling drugs on the streets.

Brandon had gotten to know John's family fairly well from work he was doing in the community. He saw firsthand a lot of the poor family dynamics within John's family that drove him to the streets. To help, he often spoke with John about life issues and being a productive citizen.

One summer, John's family needed to move but didn't have anywhere to go in-between homes. Since Brandon had become good friends with the family, he offered for John to stay with him for a few days. The few days soon became a few weeks because John's mother was arrested for an active warrant. Brandon didn't want John to go back to the streets, and his other family members were staying with friends, so Brandon decided he would let John stay longer. During this time he made sure John got to school and stayed out of trouble.

John's mother eventually got out of jail, and John returned home. Immediately, John began getting in trouble again and missing school. John told Brandon that he wanted to do better but he felt as if he had to make his own way in the world. Upon hearing this, Brandon offered for John to stay with him, with the stipulation that he must go to school and stay out of trouble. John agreed and made great effort to keep his word.

Brandon did not allow John to stay out all night, do drugs, or skip school. When John would try to do these prohibited behaviors, Brandon would consistently give him guidance and encouragement, and set the example by his own behavior.

John hadn't seen his biological father since he was six and had no real memories of him. Brandon displayed for John an example of what a productive male can do without being a deadbeat, drug dealer, or criminal. John ended up staying with Brandon for the next five years. During that time John had the typical teenage opposition, but he kept his promise of staying out of trouble and staying in school. Today John is in college working on his associate's degree. Clearly, the influence Brandon provided and sense of family he instilled in John turned John's life around and gave him direction. Without it, John might have likely been just another statistic.

*****

## Kevin

Kevin's mother was one of Brandon's very good friends from high school. When Kevin was born, she and her fiancé (Kevin's father), asked Brandon to be Kevin's Godfather. Brandon gladly accepted this honor and was looking forward to being a part of Kevin's life.

Kevin's mother and father were planning a lavish wedding ceremony, but two weeks before the wedding Kevin's father was arrested for warrants from drug charges, armed robbery, and carjacking. This was the turning point at which Brandon became much more than the typical ceremonial Godparent.

Kevin's mother took the arrest extremely hard. She became depressed, withdrawn, and isolated. Most days she sat in her apartment without leaving, and Kevin was becoming an extremely fretful baby. Brandon started going to get Kevin every weekend, which would include fun outings and church. Soon the weekend outing became a daily one, as he would pick Kevin up from day care and keep him until his mother got off work.

By all accounts, Brandon became a surrogate dad. He potty trained Kevin, watched him take his first steps, checked homework, went to school programs, and provided discipline when needed. Early on, Kevin even gave Brandon the title of "Daddy."

By the time Kevin was nine years old, his biological father was released and jailed three times. Aside from Brandon, a grandfather, and an uncle, Kevin had few positive male role models.

Kevin's mother eventually got back on track, became an R.N., and regained her emotional stability. While Kevin's mother becoming stable definitely added to Kevin's overall enrichment, Brandon believes his influence over the boy and commitment to give the boy a sense of family also played a huge part. Brandon took Kevin under his wing because he knew that with his mother being in turmoil early on, Kevin was a child at risk of becoming a statistic. He didn't want that to happen, and since he didn't have kids of his own he had the time and resources to be a benefit to Kevin.

Today Kevin is a "B" student in the second grade. He is a very polite and respectful boy who is appreciative of what he has. Kevin has much more growing to do, but he is on the right track. Without the positive influence of Brandon, Kevin's story might have been much different.

*****

What's important to note about both instances of influence is that Brandon functioned just like a "real family" is supposed to function in the boys' lives. He was in it for the long haul. Brandon wasn't attempting to be an "in and out" quick fix. He started the process and saw it through all the ups and downs. This is important, because if you start this process of influence and don't see it through, you could add to the child's perception that ALL adults are untrustworthy.

## True Support versus Toxic Love

Brandon is the prime example of true support. This is in stark contrast to the toxic love so many children experience while growing up—myself included. My father was the prime example of toxic love. He was always putting me down, and he wanted me to fail and to conform to his ideas about who we were as a family. My father could also be cruel. He could cut me down with a word just when I was congratulating myself for a small success.

Now that I'm grown, I'm able to see how human he was in his failings, how sad he was because he couldn't overcome his jealous and controlling instincts, and how his attitude hurt him as much as it hurt his family. I can see how, in the end, he left this earth without ever having truly enjoyed his wife, his children, or his grandchildren. We always wanted to love him—to create a true sense of family—but he never knew how to love us.

Today, I know that my father set me up to fail. He set me a test I couldn't pass. He didn't want to know who I was or what I wanted; he just wanted me down there in the dumps with him. That's toxic love.

But, like John and Kevin, I found other supporters—others who could help me learn what a sense of family meant. I can still remember my grandmother, my father's mother, going nose to nose with her son on my behalf. He was 30 years younger than her and a good foot taller, but she didn't let that stop her. My father had just told me, yet again, "You'll never amount to anything!" when suddenly my grandmother appeared. She walked right up to him, stuck a finger in his chest and said, "You leave that child alone. She's okay." Then, right in front of him, she turned to me and said, "Don't you listen to him. You can do anything!" At that moment, that tiny old woman was larger than life. She was my champion. She was 10 feet tall.

I was blessed to have such a strong woman in my life to influence me when my father could not. My grandmother enabled me to see that my father's criticisms didn't have to define me.

My grandmother understood the importance of honesty in relationships. My grandmother loved her son, but she never failed to stand up to him and tell him when he was doing wrong, when he was hurting his children. She loved him, but with an honest love that was able to see his flaws and speak the truth about them. My father may not have benefited from her honest feedback, because he didn't listen. But I did, and it helped me establish the beginnings of self-esteem and a sense of family, enough to build on, so that I could build a future. As I got older, I learned to create my own family of support, outside my family of origin.

The great tragedy of my father's life—and the great obstacle that I have had to overcome in my own—is the fact that he was never able to see that instead of being supportive to his family, he was poisoning us with self-doubt. He wanted to love us but he never learned how, even though the model was right in front of him.

Even today, I only choose to surround myself with people I can trust, and I take my network of supporters seriously. I also have to always trust myself to choose the right people. Trusting myself is often an uphill battle. I come back, time and again, to the image of my grandmother poking her finger in my father's chest and telling him he was wrong about me. I was blessed to have her in my life, but I also have to make the choice, again and again, to listen to her voice instead of to his.

God bless my grandmother, my elementary teacher Mrs. Kaufman, and Brandon. God bless all those people who have the vision to look at others and see not "just another statistic." God bless those people who see the potential and who influence and nurture it—just like a real family should.

## A Family Affair

If you're a parent, it's your job to instill a sense of family in your children. If you're not a parent, you can instill a sense of family in the young people in your life. You, too, can become a child's support system as she struggles to overcome toxic love and find her path to success.

Instilling a strong sense of family is more important these days than ever before. Why? Because today's children face an even greater obstacle course of challenges on their road to responsible, successful adulthood than just a generation ago. Today more media is available—indeed, un-avoidable—than ever before. Technology has changed our children's world irrevocably. One result is that children grow up much more quickly. Younger children mimic the behavior of older teenagers, in a way making them their family. You see younger and younger children wearing suggestive clothing, adopting foul and suggestive language, engaging in sexual activity, and on down the list. The media increases their awareness of this once-forbidden world.

Media overload puts a burden on parents and adults that wasn't there a generation ago. Teaching children to value the things that are important to the family is much more difficult now because they're overwhelmed on a daily basis with advertising messages urging them to enjoy short-term pleasures at the expense of long-term learning and discipline. They're bombarded with technological toys that connect them to a world that can distract them from the priorities of education and exercise, family and friendships. They meet each other via Facebook, My Space, Twitter, and texting. They listen to iPods and play Guitar Hero. They watch nonstop cable TV.

Yet children must acquire more knowledge than ever to be considered educated by modern standards. The learning curve is growing steeper at the same time as the temptations to take a wrong turn—or just a lazy turn—have become more numerous and sophisticated.

It's not an easy time to be a parent, a concerned adult, or a child.

In the face of this, some parents give up and pursue their own selfish ends. Too many parents today are simply not involved in their children's lives or not providing the proper influence. Discipline and guidance suffer when parents are absent. When parents are available, but insufficiently mature to handle responsibility, their children often suffer abuse or neglect.

Yet the fundamentals remain the same as ever: parenting has never been easy. There never has been a handy, simple rulebook to teach parents how to influence in an ever-evolving world.

I see all these issues playing out every day in my work in the behavioral healthcare field. Sometimes the parents are present, but they don't take the time they should to nurture, influence, and discipline their kids.

Often, parents are absent. Single parent families are all too common, and many grandmothers have taken on the exhausting task of raising their children's children.

What's the solution?

First, parents and adults must commit to becoming more involved. There is no shortcut to parenting. If you're a parent, you have to put in the time. If other responsibilities and interests are competing for your attention, you must prioritize: your children must top your list. Teach them to use good judgment and to make good decisions. If you're not the parent, then get involved in youth activities in the community. Your involvement can make a world of difference in a child's life.

Second, you need to know how your children are doing in school. Be active in the school system. Get to know their teachers. Teachers and administrators are longing for more positive parental involvement. Working closely with your child's teacher is one way to build a healthy network of caring and concerned adults. This positive influence not only affects your child, but indirectly affects other kids who experience this type of interaction in the classroom.

Third, you need to know who your children's friends are, and what they're doing with those friends. Find out how they spend their leisure time. I often see young parents who want to be friends with their kids, so their kids will like them or maybe even think they're "cool." But that doesn't make for good influence. Kids want and need structure and discipline. Parents or other adults must provide that for them. You have to be willing to be your kid's "enemy" for a day or two if you're going to be a good parent.

Children fear chaos, and there's too much of that in their world today.

Of course I see children every day at Edgewater, and I hear them talk about the issues that are upsetting them. Today's kids feel increasingly isolated and alienated in a world of single parents, working parents, latchkey kids, play-dates, Internet friendships, and microwave dinners. Like earlier generations, they feel the adults around them aren't listening to them. Unlike earlier generations, there are many more competing demands for a parent's attention, making it harder to find time to pay attention to our kids. Sometimes children expect too much from us, but sometimes our children are right: sometimes we're not really listening.

We need to listen, now as much as ever. We need to ask our children what's on their minds, what's bothering them, what they're happy about, what their hopes and fears are. When we stop listening, it's not only tragic for children who may be lonelier than we realize—it's also a recipe for disaster. Children need a sounding board, someone who is concerned about them and willing to listen. But adults need to listen and respond as role models, not buddies. Children need to know we hear their problems, but they also need to trust that we can provide solutions that come from a world of experience beyond their own. A peer can't do that; only an adult role model can.

When young people feel they've been heard, they're more likely to follow rules and grow up perceiving that they have a stake in society. They're more likely to become good citizens.

Kids struggle with rejection and peer pressure, bullying and fighting, gangs and violence. They need a sense of family so they can cope with the harsher realities of modern life. Many kids know loss much earlier than was typical a generation ago. They lose peers to the streets, homelessness, drugs, and gang violence. They know death early, and they need help to cope.

They need to learn how to control their impulses. They need experienced adults to prepare them to cope with the world. A lot of families are dealing with internal problems of alcohol or drug abuse, mental and emotional problems, and sexual abuse. Families working to recover from these issues need to help their children learn to spot the signs of those problems in themselves, their other family members, and their friends. They need to learn what to do when confronting dysfunctional situations. Children who live in dysfunctional families and who aren't on their way to recovery need strong adult mentors outside their families. They need mature adults to help them learn the signs of trouble, to give them tools to protect themselves, and to teach them how to find support systems and organizations that can help.

In our rush to see kids grow up and take on their share of family and community responsibilities, we can easily forget that children have limited verbal and emotional processing skills that limit the quality of their decision-making—even in their teens, when they seem so much like little adults. They're still just kids! They need a chance to have a childhood.

Children and teens have so much to learn, it can be overwhelming, such as:

- How to handle confrontation, crises, and threats

- How to communicate

- How to control impulses

- How to cope with the ups and downs of everyday life

- How to be resilient—how to bounce back from trauma, pressures, or stress

- How to set goals and take action on them to become successful

Having a strong sense of family is the first step to youth learning these things. Additionally, realize that it is not the responsibility of schools to teach these things, nor can they do so effectively. Children learn to overcome challenges and set goals through role modeling by adults and through personal experience. Children need parents to not only tell them what to do, but to show them what to do, and to support them when they must do it on their own.

Even some of the most well-intentioned parents neglect their kids, fail to discipline them, or don't provide much needed encouragement because they're overwhelmed and have no idea how to cope with their own problems. Parents have troubles of their own—financial pressures, career issues, marital problems—and all of these issues make it hard to take the time and thought necessary to be a good parent or role model. This has to change; otherwise, a greater proportion of tomorrow's adults will grow up with a skewed view of the world. They'll see it as cruel and uncaring, and in response they'll learn to be alienated and isolated. They'll end up as bullies, dropouts, or suicides, either in their teen years or down the road as life continues to unload on them and they continue to feel unable to respond.

Not all parents will rise to this occasion. That's why all adults need to be involved. We can't let these things happen to our children's future, which will also be, at least for a time, our future.

If you're a parent or role model to a child, always be on the lookout for the warning signs of trouble—the signs that the child is floundering with no sense of where to turn: a sudden change in clothes, sudden change in eating or sleeping habits, sudden drop in grades, hanging out with bad kids, not listening or paying attention, frequent dubious illnesses. Constant isolation, anger, depression—all of those are signs of trouble. This is why it's important to talk to and listen to children before these problems begin. You can't spot a change in a child unless you know plenty about him in the first place.

Fundamentally, we have to set limits for our kids, because they won't do it themselves. We have to demand that they follow the rules and provide real consequences if they break them.

Resist the temptation to insist that your child start acting like an adult. Introduce your children to the grown-up world as slowly as possible. They're going to be adults soon enough. Let them be kids while they can. In fact, insist upon it—if they have more time to develop into adults, they will have a stronger foundation to become responsible, successful adults.

Encourage your children to try hard. Don't be satisfied with mediocrity. It's important to encourage them to do their best. The world is competitive, and they need to know how to deal with that. Effort leads to success, and they need to learn not to shy away from effort. That's not to say you should break their spirit when they do their best and don't win. That could contribute to an inferiority complex. Again, this is why it's important to get to know your child, so you'll know when she's actually trying her best and be able to give her credit for it. The best way to teach kids how to be successful in life is to get your own house in order. As long as they're the kids, then we're the role models. It's our job to raise them safely and well.

And most of all, let children be themselves. Don't unduly burden them with your expectations. Too many parents raise kids with all the expectations they once had for their own lives, or burden their kids with the need to make up for all the things they never had: "My kid is going to be a star, or a football player, or a lawyer, because I was, or because I wasn't." Either way, it's a form of selfishness that puts a burden on the kid when it's tough enough for him already.

Give your kids a safe environment, and the space and support to become their own best selves. It's not easy, but that's the job you signed up for when you became a parent. Or, if you're not a parent but you want to help instill a sense of family in the children you encounter, that's the job you can sign up for. When you help influence the life of a child, you make this a better world for all of them and everyone whose lives they touch.

# Chapter Four

# Influence Youth to Adopt Healthy Habits

*"It is health that is real wealth and not pieces of gold and silver."*
~ Mohandas Gandhi

No one wants to see children, many of whom are already overweight, growing into obese, lethargic adults destined for a slew of health problems, many of which can be prevented. Yet the problem keeps growing.

According to the Centers for Disease Control and Prevention (CDC) in 2008, the percentage of children aged 6-11 years in the United States who were obese increased from 7% in 1980 to nearly 20% in 2008. Similarly, adolescents aged 12 to 19 who were obese went from 5% to 18% during the same period. Since 1980, obesity prevalence among children and adolescents has tripled, and in 2008 more than one third of the nation's children and adolescents were obese or overweight. Additionally, there are significant racial and ethnic disparities in obesity prevalence among U.S. children and adolescents. For example, Hispanic boys aged 2 to 19 years are significantly more likely to be obese than non-Hispanic white boys, and non-Hispanic black girls are significantly more likely to be obese than non-Hispanic white girls.

Why should this be a concern to parents and adults? Because childhood obesity has many consequences that reach far beyond the biological family. For example, overweight and obese children are more likely to have:

- High blood pressure and high cholesterol, which are risk factors for cardiovascular disease (CVD). In one study, 70% of obese children had at least one CVD risk factor, and 39% had two or more.

- Increased risk of impaired glucose tolerance, insulin resistance, and Type 2 diabetes.

- Breathing problems, such as sleep apnea and asthma.

- Joint problems and musculoskeletal discomfort.

- Fatty liver disease, gallstones, and gastro-esophageal reflux (i.e., heartburn).

Additionally, obese children and adolescents have a greater risk of social and psychological problems, such as discrimination and poor self-esteem, which can continue into adulthood.

Speaking of adulthood, obese children are more likely to become obese adults. And adult obesity is associated with a number of serious health conditions including heart disease, diabetes, and some cancers. Even more alarming, if children are overweight, obesity in adulthood is likely to be more severe.

Unfortunately, even when a family has many choices of what food to bring into the house, some young parents don't have the information or experience to make good ones. Some young mothers don't understand that giving children donuts for breakfast will make it harder for them to concentrate in school, or that skipping vegetables may weaken their child's immune system. All those young mothers know is that they have to get to work early, or stay at work late, and donuts and mac-and-cheese are easy and cheap. Cold cereals might be easy, but an ill-educated parent might not understand how to read labels and end up with a cereal as sugary and unhealthful as donuts. Mom and Dad might be able to afford veggies, but may not know how to prepare them so their kids will eat them. Many of these habits stubbornly resist change.

Running a behavioral health facility in Gary, Indiana, I see far too many people—adults and children—who suffer physical and mental health problems associated with poor nutrition and lack of exercise. I see obesity and diabetes, depression and anxiety, and increased susceptibility to viruses and infections. These conditions affect me as an employer as well: I see more absenteeism and less productivity. Not only do these trends financially impact our organization, but they also hit our entire community with increased health care costs and lost productivity. They leave many young people floundering, unable to succeed at school or to find and keep good jobs.

Our clients typically see us to deal with mental health issues, not physical issues. But more and more we're beginning to deal with their physical healthcare needs as well. That's because mental illness and physical illness go hand-in-hand. People with chronic mental illness typically have such conditions as increased blood pressure, diabetes, heart disease, and cardiopulmonary disease. Their medications may create other medical problems. For example, doctors commonly prescribe Haldol or Prolixin to treat schizophrenia, but these two medications can sometimes cause Tardive Dyskinesia (TD), a rare, but serious and sometimes permanent side effect characterized by twitching or jerking movements that a person cannot control in his   face, tongue, or other parts of the body. Consequently, it is important to understand that creating healthy individuals means being aware of a person's total healthcare needs, both mental and physical, and ensuring that these needs are met with appropriate and timely treatment.

## A National Health Crisis

Today we're facing a national epidemic: childhood obesity. At a time when medical care is growing more expensive we can't afford to be fat. Obesity contributes to and worsens almost all other health problems. Sadly, obesity is preventable, yet it seems we lack the public will to tackle it. However, parents and other concerned adults can take steps to help the youth in their lives make healthy choices so they can lead healthy and productive lives, and not end up as statistics.

How did everyone, including today's youth, get so fat? We have become a less physically active society. Schools have cut back on physical education programs. Children don't play outside as much because their parents fear for their safety. Often they enjoy modern technology instead: computers, TV, video games, iPods, and texting. More moms work today, and one unintended consequence is that more kids eat more fast food, junk food, and quick-fix packaged foods. Add all those ingredients together and you have a recipe for millions of overfed couch potatoes. The result? Obesity.

I sometimes pick up my young grandson from school. Javier is always hungry, and where does he want to go? McDonald's. It's not even the food he wants so much as the toys; the food simply comes with them. Even with my education and experience, I find it difficult to compete with the relentless marketing. How much more difficult must it be for an exhausted 20-year-old mother who may work at a fast-food counter herself?

How can we influence our children so they can escape this perfect storm of trends? We need to promote good health as relentlessly as Domino's promotes pizza—the common currency of colleges and universities. But first we need to recognize that good health is not going to be as easy a sell as pizza. We need a game plan. We need to start that game plan in our own homes.

It's not enough to just say "no" to kids. They're way too smart and wily for that. As parents, grandparents, and mentors, if we're going to fight obesity we need to give kids alternatives that make sense to them.

Kids deal with stress and peer pressure. We need to give them ways to deal with those issues, as well as to connect with health and wellness. Exercise, not eating, I've found, is the cure to just about everything. Kids should be walking, riding bikes, and getting more exercise generally. I'm convinced that much of what we classify as attention deficit disorder would go away if children just got much more exercise and ate less sugar than they do now.

Parents and all adults for that matter have a responsibility here and an opportunity to influence. They need to spend face time with kids talking to them about good health, exercise, and nutrition. They also need to model the good behavior they're preaching about. Mom can't just say, "Here, have a carrot stick," while she eats her bag of chips. Parents have to find ways to make it fun to eat healthy and fun to exercise—both for themselves and their children. Here are a few ideas:

- A raw carrot might not be tasty, a cooked carrot might be mushy, but stir-fry some carrots and broccoli with beef and soy sauce and, "Guess what kids? Tonight we're eating Chinese!"

- Does your kid like spaghetti? Add some different colored veggies to the sauce. Maybe he won't like all of them, but he might like one of them. If he's old enough, maybe he can help wash them or chop them. Getting involved in the preparation of healthful, attractive food might make him more engaged in eating it.

- Does your neighborhood have a community garden? Maybe he can learn to plant his own cabbages, and then eat a salad he helped grow.

The same goes for exercise. You have to give kids alternatives. Doing push-ups might be boring, and going out to run around the neighborhood might be dangerous, but maybe the local YMCA or Boys and Girls Club has a basketball court or a gymnastics class where your daughter can play and learn with other children her age.

Society as a whole needs to think through these issues, and create programs and approaches that make more sense. For example, why is it so hard to serve healthful food in institutional settings or schools? I've been in far too many hospitals where the luncheon served is fried chicken, mashed potatoes, and gravy, and too many schools rely on pizza as a lunch staple. These may have been respectable meals 50 years ago, but we know too much now to serve stupid stuff like that! This is where all adults can speak up and wield some influence in the matter.

According to the American Diabetes Association's 2011 Fact Sheet, 25.8 million children and adults in the United States—8.3% of the population—have diabetes. Did you know that diabetes alone cost this country $174 billion in 2007? Yet most of that problem would go away if we were a fitter nation.

Sometimes it's too late for prevention, and not all illnesses can be prevented. Even then, receiving early diagnosis and care is healthier and less expensive than waiting. Yet our medical system often punishes those of us who are proactive and rewards those who wait. Society needs to come up with some way to ensure that services are provided in a cost-effective manner. Our insurance system is designed to respond to particular health-threatening events, rather than long-term health promotion. So it's easier to wait for a diabetic to undergo an expensive leg amputation than it is to enroll her in an inexpensive obesity management class. That makes no sense for the woman, who could have saved her leg, and it makes no sense for the rest of us who have to pay higher insurance premiums—or forego insurance altogether due to the expense.

## The Interconnectedness of It All

At Edgewater, in our chronic population—people who have suffered mental illness for many years—we see many interrelated medical problems. There's definitely a connection between hypertension and smoking. For many years the accepted wisdom was, "Why take their cigarettes away? It's the only pleasure they have."

Now we know that if we want to encourage people to take control of their lives, we have to encourage them to get a handle on the behaviors and habits that negatively affect not only their mental health, but also their physical health. Smoking is one of those habits. But how do you successfully convince people who are chronically ill to quit smoking, eat less, exercise more, and focus on healthier choices? It's not easy. They've heard it all before, and often a stubborn attitude is either a contributing factor or a symptom of their mental and/or physical problems.

Children who come to us are in an even more difficult position. They struggle with behavior problems that are interfering with their growth into healthy, functioning adults. Children typically stay with us for only a small amount of time. They still face challenges when they leave, and they must deal with those challenges in the midst of overloaded public schools, at home with overwhelmed parents, and in the company of friends and peers who put tremendous pressure on them to conform. Sometimes peers reject them due to their behavioral problems; other times peers pressure them to return to their former behavioral problems. We have to reach across that divide to get our message out loud and clear. It's so hard to keep them drug-free and violence-free, and sometimes it can seem an insurmountable obstacle to also keep them potato chip-free and soda pop-free.

Yet why bother helping children overcome cycles of violence and substance abuse only to let them grow into obese, lethargic adults destined for the mental and physical health problems that go along with that? We can't save kids from one problem only to throw them away on another. Kids must understand the importance of healthy lifestyles. We must make it clear to them that eating fat and sugar and lazing on the couch, which may seem easy, will ultimately lead them into unhappy lives.

All adults have an obligation to provide kids with the information and skills they need to lead them to successful lives. Someone needs to tell them that success doesn't just mean getting good grades or a good job; it's also about achieving happiness and fulfillment and a sense of well-being. That kind of success is not possible without a healthy lifestyle.

But learning healthy lifestyles is part of societal conditioning. So unless communities teach these values as a collaborative effort, as a community of adults all working together, we're fighting an uphill battle to influence our unhealthy youth.

As a society, we need to speak out for a more sensible health care system. Yet whatever we do and say in the battle to influence the youth of our communities, we must still sow the seeds for change at home. We each must give nutritious food and exercise primary roles in a healthy lifestyle. And it's equally important for us to strike a balance between work life and home life. It is pointless to work endlessly without taking time out for family and leisure pursuits. Then life becomes meaningless, and stress-related illnesses or obesity become inevitable.

The fact is that people are more productive when they're less stressed. What I've learned to do to decrease stress in my own life is to schedule my leisure activity. I schedule it as if it's just as important as any item on my work calendar, because it is. For example, I regularly go to the gym and work out with a trainer at a pre-arranged time. Maybe you can't afford a trainer or a gym, but maybe you have a pair of running shoes or a ball. Or you can take time to walk. You may think you're too busy, but when you make exercise and fun leisure activities part of your lifestyle, you'll find you're actually more productive at everything else you do. I've discovered a paradox: when I make time for exercise, I have more time and energy for everything else in my life, not less.

## Taking Healthy Influence to a New Level

As a behavioral specialist, I've seen firsthand the cost to our community when we fail to treat health and wellness as a priority. But don't just take my word for it. Consider it from the viewpoint of a medical expert. Dr. Steve Simpson is a pediatrician whose selfless service to promote the health and welfare of children and families has helped make him one of Gary, Indiana's local heroes. He has definitely taken his role as an influencer of healthy choices to a new level.

Dr. Simpson was raised in Gary. He went to college in Washington D.C., at a historically black institution, where he received a degree in chemistry. He could have gone anywhere from there. But he decided to go home and become a humble pediatrician. He went to medical school at Indiana University and did his residency at a local children's hospital. With the exception of four years in the Air Force, he's been here ever since.

Dr. Simpson could have taken the road to widespread recognition and glory, but instead took the road home to service. He puts it simply: "I wanted to come back to Gary to provide health care to its residents because I knew there was a shortage. I've had my practice established in the inner city for the past 28 years."

Low-income parents like Diana couldn't be more grateful that Dr. Simpson has stayed in Gary's east side, where he has been a Godsend for many children. When Diana's daughter, Iyanna, was eight, she grew so ill she was unable to keep any food down. Terrified at her daughter's non-stop vomiting, Diana took her to a general practitioner, who referred the girl to the emergency room of a local hospital. An ER doctor diagnosed her with Type 1 diabetes and sent her to the intensive care unit. The hospital staff began looking for a specialist to treat Iyanna, but they had trouble finding anyone who was immediately available.

Diana grew increasingly worried until a nurse, seeing her fear, suggested an easier option: "Just get a good pediatrician. He should know what to do." Diana had never been able to afford to regularly take her children to a pediatrician, and she only knew of one: the man who had circumcised her son 20 years earlier, Dr. Simpson.

The nurse contacted Dr. Simpson for her. He came in at the first possible moment and ran tests on Iyanna. Then he met with Diana, who was crying. "Girl, wipe your tears," he said. "Everything's going to be all right." As the doctor explained her daughter's problem and the prescribed treatment, his down to earth manner melted her fears.

Iyanna is now entering her early teens and doing quite well. The medical treatment Dr. Simpson provided and the lifestyle changes he recommended have made a remarkable difference in her health. A family doctor who takes his calling seriously, he makes himself a part of his patients' lives. He often calls to check on Iyanna's blood sugar levels, and always makes himself 100 percent available to answer Diana's questions. Not only that, but he shows an interest in the entire family's well-being—not just as patients, but as friends. He has even invited them to his home to meet his own family. The words "bedside manner" don't even begin to cover it.

Diana calls Dr. Simpson a "drum major" among physicians, an example they all should follow. He deflects such praise the same way he puts patients at ease: by reminding them that he's just a man from the projects, himself. "I'm just a man whom God has blessed," he says.

His unassuming attitude, and his inspiring rise from his humble neighborhood, only make his patients love and appreciate him more.

As a drum major, there is one topic on which this usually quiet man pounds a loud and constant beat: Dr. Simpson says one of the primary health threats to the next generation is the inner city epidemic of young people having babies. They're just not ready for the responsibility. "Until you're about 25, you think like a child. Adolescent parents face a tremendous burden, trying to raise children themselves."

Dr. Simpson faces daily challenges from patients who fail to take responsibility for themselves or their children. "We have a 50 percent no-show rate (for patients)," he says. "In any other business, you'd go out of business with that kind of dropout rate. And we're talking about life and death—getting your kids vaccinated, that sort of thing. All too often, parents just don't get it. They don't understand that if they don't bring their baby in now, the kid will get sick later."

I ask Dr. Simpson about recent trends in health care. He echoes my thoughts, saying we are focusing our attention in the wrong direction. "If you believe the diagnoses, we have an epidemic of ADD (Attention Deficit Disorder) and ADHD (Attention Deficit Hyperactivity Disorder). Personally, I think the diseases are over-diagnosed. They're coming in from the schools. The teachers used to tolerate that behavior more, I think. Now they won't take it, and they send more kids in for drugs to calm them down."

That's treating the symptoms, but not the underlying causes. That's neither prevention nor cure, but a stopgap measure that does nothing to prevent the spiral of never-ending academic and social problems for the misdiagnosed child. Sometimes what these over-active, inattentive children really need is more involved parents and smaller class sizes so that they have more opportunities to express themselves and their interests, and feel less need to act out. Sometimes they need more physical activity and a healthier diet to promote energy and focus. What they need most is for parents to pay attention to their mental and physical needs before problems develop. What they need is a preventative approach to health and wellness.

## What We All Can Do to Influence Healthy Habits

Dr Simpson believes that the key to helping the next generation improve their health is to improve their education. The three R's are just a beginning. They need to learn what "health" really means. "It's the usual things—exercising and eating properly. That would help with obesity, diabetes, and hypertension, all the diseases I see in adults. And the sad fact is that I see more and more of those three in kids, too."

But education is not free. If any community wants to see the benefits of a total approach to education, it's going to take a strong application of public will. There's a Catch-22 here: many of the people who need education the most don't know enough yet to fight for it. Those who have enough education to understand the need must step into the breach and either stand up for those who can't, or teach them to stand up for themselves, or teach at least one person what he or she needs to know to infect the rest—with knowledge.

"Gary has a good opportunity for recovery. If our political issues are resolved, Gary has great resources. We lack a strategic plan for health care. In previous times there was a group of people meeting to determine how Gary's health care system was going to look. That kind of thinking has not been occurring for the past 15 years because of a lack of coordinated leadership. We need new, strong leadership from someone who has a vision for improving healthcare for all our citizens. And that goes for all America."

Many Americans voted for President Barack Obama because he spoke about these types of solutions. But he, too, has emphasized the need for everyone to get involved. Even the best leaders cannot save us unless we work to save ourselves and to help each other.

Some of the problems facing our communities are daunting. "We're seeing a rash of infants born to mothers addicted to drugs," Dr. Simpson says. "And the drugs have changed. It used to be crack and cocaine, now it's methamphetamines." It can be tough to figure out how to help children who seem doomed from the womb. But with more education, we can expect fewer drug-addicted teens.

There are some problems that communities have always had that they continue to have. Dr. Simpson sees plenty of kids with ear infections, problems in school, and unstable families. Yet these problems too can diminish under the influence of education. Clearly, education and health go hand in hand.

Like me, Dr. Simpson believes we should not only teach children academics, physical education, and health, but we should also train teens and young adults who plan to become parents, who accidentally become parents, or who just might become parents someday. "If I had an opportunity to talk to a young couple I'd talk to them about the responsibility of parenting. Most of us go to school to learn how to get a job—not how to be parents. We are not trained to be parents. It's trial and error. Parents would benefit enormously from learning something about early childhood development."

Dr. Simpson believes that if we started there, if we just trained people to become better parents, so many health and education challenges could be avoided. "They would look differently at the school system—they would see that they need to be part of it. They would teach their kids to become part of the community—to contribute, not be a parasite. And that would affect all the problems I see every day in my practice."

Dr. Simpson has seen it all in nearly three decades of practicing pediatric medicine. So perhaps we would be wise to give our children his prescription for influence. By doing our part to promote changes in education, and by starting to teach young people the importance of personal responsibility and healthy choices now, we begin the process of turning our community ills into the picture of health.

# Chapter Five

# Influence Youth to
# Make Smart Decisions about Sex

*"Sex education, including its spiritual aspects, should be part of a
broad health and moral education from kindergarten through grade
twelve, ideally carried out harmoniously by parents and teachers."*
~ Benjamin Spock, *Dr. Spock's Baby and Child Care*

Sex is a tough subject to talk about. But we need to be more open
about it, if only to help our children combat the epidemic of teenage
pregnancy in this country.

It used to be that kids played outside in their yards, and even on
their neighborhood streets, secure in the illusion that as long as they
stayed close to home they were safe. Today many parents keep their
kids locked indoors, afraid a sex fiend might grab them. It's an almost
universal perception that the world is much more dangerous than it
was a generation ago.

That's the perception. But is it real?

The reality is a complicated mixture of better, worse, and bad news
as usual.

- **Worse:** Thanks mainly to the Internet, there are new forms
  of crimes against children that didn't exist just 15 years ago.
  As technology has opened the door to more opportunities in
  business, information, and social networking, it has also
  opened the door to new opportunities for thieves, sexual
  predators, and unsupervised teens with undeveloped

decision-making skills. The Internet has provided new means for child predators to stalk their prey, and for children to engage in adult behavior with each other.

- **Worse:** Teens are having sex at younger ages than ever. According to self-reporting by teens, drinking and drugs are playing a greater role than ever in the choice to engage in underage sex.

- **Bad news as usual:** Conventional criminals have long targeted children at a higher rate than adults, simply because children are more vulnerable and make easier victims. According to the Crimes Against Children Research Center (CACRC) at the University of New Hampshire, *children become victims of rape, robbery, and assault substantially more often than adults do.*

- **Bad news as usual:** Children also suffer a disproportionate burden of victimization in the home—physical abuse, sexual abuse, emotional abuse, and neglect.

- **Better:** Sex abuse and physical abuse crimes against children appear to be declining overall. According to the CACRC, *substantiated cases of child sexual abuse went down 51% from 1990 to 2005; physical abuse substantiations declined 46% between 1992 and 2005; sexual assaults on teenagers decreased by 52% from 1993 to 2005. Other crimes against children 12 to 17 years old have also declined.*

- **Better:** Parents are increasingly aware of crimes against children, crimes by children, and the risky behaviors in which even model children engage—such as drinking and drug use, meeting strangers on the Internet, and engaging in teen sex.

For better or worse, statistics mean little when you're worried about your own child becoming a victim. In a world of expanded information, any responsible adult would try to do more to keep children safe from the evils all around.

Neither the idyllic illusion of a safer past, nor the chronic fear of a dangerous present, is completely based in fact. It's good that we're more aware today of the dangers our children face, and we should be vigilant about protecting them. But we need to balance common sense supervision with giving our children a long enough leash so they can get outdoors and exercise, do things on their own and develop independence, and learn to socialize with peers. And we need to remember that protecting our children from predators is not enough—often the biggest danger to our children is a failure to protect them from themselves.

## Stranger Danger

Should we teach children to steer clear of strangers? Of course. But I'm sorry to say that small children are easy to fool. Studies have shown that no matter how clearly you teach them to say "no," if a stranger says something like, "Your mommy is hurt, and she asked me to come get you," many children will still follow that person off the playground. Don't let that panic you. Small children can still play outside in relative safety while a trusted neighborhood adult sits on the porch watching, or in the backyard of a friend whose parents are home, or at many after-school programs.

When children get older, it gets more complicated. We need to be frank with them about just what can happen if they fail to say "no," not just to strangers but to people they know.

Often it's easier to demonize the influences of the outside world and try to keep our children locked inside. But even inside, TVs, iPods, the Internet, and bedrooms without 24-hour surveillance cameras pose risks. Sexual imagery abounds even on PG-rated TV programs and non-explicit iPod downloads. Sexual predators surf the social networks pretending to be fellow teens. And in an age of more single parents and working parents, peer pressure trumps parental pressure when it comes to sex, drugs, late nights, overloaded cars, and dangerous places.

If we want to protect our kids, we have to protect them from their own ignorance. While we don't want to make them terrified that the world is full of evil boogeymen, they should know enough facts about the dangers out there so that they have a better chance to avoid people and situations that could harm them. Even more imperative: we must arm them with the information that will help them make good choices when they interact with their peers.

## Educate for Influence

The key is for adults to influence our youth so they don't become dysfunctional victims.

Influence them so they move toward strong futures.

Influence them so we decrease teen pregnancies, which only contribute to cycles of poverty, abuse, and neglect.

Influence them so we decrease sexually transmitted diseases (STDs), which can impair health, lead to sterility, or even cause death.

Influence them so they can recognize and avoid predators.

Influence them so they can avoid choices that take them off the path to healthy relationships, good educations, and bright futures.

How do we start this sort of influence? We start by battling America's near-phobic reluctance to talk about sex. As with most community issues, this is one we must begin at home.

You may find it tough to talk about sex. Many of us have been socialized to think of sex as dirty, embarrassing, or funny. Some of us have been victims of abuse or our own bad choices. Some of us have religious beliefs about sex that we want to defend. But whatever your political views, religion, experience, or beliefs, sexuality is healthy and human. If we don't talk about sex we run the risk of letting it devolve into something unhealthy, or even inhuman. If we don't talk about it, our kids will find a way to talk about it anyway. Do we really want them leading that conversation on their own?

If America's adults don't start talking to kids about sex, America's kids will continue to pay the price. And believe me, they already are paying a price. Here in the Midwest we're seeing an alarming trend of teen girls getting pregnant by increasingly older males, often three to six years older than they are. Here in Indiana, the teen birth rate has begun to rise over the past two years, after several years without an increase. We don't yet know exactly why, although drinking and drugs are often involved. Whatever the root causes are, it's a worrying trend.

When a teenage girl gets pregnant, the options for her and her child fall down one by one, like a dreadful lineup of dominos. The father is not likely to stay around, leaving an already ill-equipped single mother to give birth and raise a child alone. The mother is likely to drop out of school and take the first in an endless series of low-income jobs. The child is more likely to be sickly, to have trouble in school, and to earn a lower income when he grows up.

As the old joke goes: just one night of sex can ruin your whole life. When it comes to sex, teenagers have all the hormones and parts required to play at adult behavior, but none of the judgment to understand the long-term consequences of engaging in adult behavior too soon. These days most teens know a lot about sex, but they don't understand much about long-term consequences. That's just not a teen strong suit. That's why adults must help stand between them and bad choices. And since we can't always be there to stand between them, our influence has to stand in for us. We have to talk to our kids.

Unfortunately, many parents avoid the subject of sex, especially with their children. And many politicians fail to support sex education because their constituents prefer to live with the fantasy that talking to teens about sex only encourages them—and that if we just don't encourage them, they won't do it. That theory hasn't worked so far. How many more young people do we want to doom to teen parenthood, academic failure, and a lifetime of poverty before we decide to admit what teenagers are up to and give them the information they need to deal with the choices they're already making without us.

Really, we're all on the same side. Conservatives or liberals, religious believers or non-believers, Republicans or Democrats: we all want teenagers to abstain from sex. If we give young people enough information, we increase the chances that more of them will abstain. And if we give them *all* the information, including information on safer sex, we increase the chances that those who choose to have sex despite our best advice might at least avoid adding sexually transmitted diseases and teen pregnancy into the mix.

Here at Edgewater, we lead "Girl Talk" sessions that focus on preadolescent and adolescent girls. A therapist leads the group sessions. But to introduce the girls to a sense of responsibility, we give them the opportunity to co-lead the program. The therapist guides them as they talk through the minefield of adult issues that young girls face, such as dating, sexuality, and drugs.

We also support a common school program you've probably heard of, in which young adolescents receive a doll that is equipped to cry when it needs to be fed, changed, or rocked to sleep. The student keeps the doll for a week, getting up for midnight "feedings," figuring out how to get through daily routines while carrying a baby, and generally suffering all the inconveniences of parenthood. The kid keeps a diary for that week and at the end discusses what the experience was like. As corny as it sounds, young teens always find this program enlightening!

We believe many of them are scared into abstinence, or at least birth control.

These programs tend to focus on girls, because when teen girls get pregnant they usually end up raising the baby alone. However, we try to work with boys at an early age, as well. The group setting isn't always as effective with boys; however, we've had good results with groups led by men who focus on mentoring boys in all the aspects of what it takes to grow to responsible manhood.

Teen pregnancy isn't the only reason we need to talk to kids about the risks and consequences of sex. Across the U.S., organizations that work with kids are seeing increasing numbers of sexually active kids with STDs. Gonorrhea and chlamydia are common, and syphilis is making an unfortunate comeback. One of the reasons for this is that teens are becoming sexually active at increasingly younger ages. It's a shocking development.

Sadly, it can be even more difficult to convince kids about the dangers of STDs than the dangers of pregnancy. Most teens have only a remote sense of mortality: they either believe they'll live forever, or they live in a world so violent that they've become numb to the fear of death. Meanwhile, kids of 12, 13, and 14 are still learning how to process information, so it can be tough to even get them to conceptualize how this information applies to them.

Yet that's all the more reason to take the time to influence and teach children about this subject. The kids can learn these things, and sooner or later the significance of it all *will* sink in. It just requires a little extra effort from the adults in their lives. It's easiest when the effort begins at home. One thing that constantly strikes people like me who work in the social service field is how simple the equation really is: kids who have more family involvement in their lives are less likely to engage in risky behaviors, period. So parents, please get involved! Don't make excuses, and don't be shy. Ask your kids what's going on.

But remember, there will always be some parents who won't get involved. So if you want to help influence today's youth, reach out and mentor just one kid in your sphere who you know lacks parental guidance. You could save that child's future, and the future of that child's children and so on.

With that said, if you want to step in and help, please be circumspect with the way you approach this. You can't just walk up to someone else's 13-year-old kid and start talking about sex. Someone could take it the wrong way; you could be seen as opposing the values of the child's parents or, in extreme cases, a pervert who just wants an excuse to talk sex with kids. Don't let that scare you off though. Find appropriate programs or channels through which to offer your time and assistance to this worthy effort.

## More Information; Better Choices

One of the biggest barriers to preventing both STDs and teen pregnancies is the controversy over explaining all birth control options to teenagers. It's a shame because, for youth who've already decided to become sexually active, sex education and contraceptives may decrease early or unplanned pregnancies.

Maybe, just maybe, if my parents had been more open with their children about sex, or had talked more to us about any subject, I would have been armed with enough information and self-esteem to help me avoid pregnancy in high school. Sex was an absolutely forbidden topic in our house. I remember a few times my older brothers would try to crack off-color jokes, but Dad would grow angry, or Mom would tell them to stop that "dirty talk." I didn't know why it was considered "dirty," because that's as far as that kind of conversation ever got. We certainly didn't have the kind of relationship with our parents in which we were invited to discuss anything in private. So that was the end of it.

Most of what I learned about my body and about sex, I learned from other kids, so I only learned distorted half-answers to half-formed questions. By the time I hit puberty I knew I was different from my brothers, and I knew that male parts were different from female parts, but the implications were lost on me.

We had a class in school called "Health and Safety," and one day the girls were taken to a separate class to learn about menstrual cycles. But after that class, I was still clueless. All I really understood was that when I started my period I would bleed, somehow, and that after that I could get pregnant if I had sex. This information was strange and confusing, and I was too embarrassed to ask for clarification.

When I had my first menstrual cycle, I freaked out. In spite of those health classes, I didn't know what was wrong with me. I knew that when a girl started her period she was supposed to bleed. But this stuff didn't look red, the way I expected blood to look. It looked brown. I was too embarrassed to tell anyone, least of all my mother, who might scold me for apparently pooping in my pants. After a couple of days of anxiety and embarrassment, I realized this messy problem wasn't going to go away. As a last resort I reluctantly went to my Mom and told her. She explained to me that it was my period, and gave me some sanitary napkins. I felt relieved.

But she still didn't talk to me about sex.

When I was a teenybopper of 11, 12, and 13, I used to read romance magazines. The books made vague references to lovemaking, which mostly consisted of men kissing women, caressing them, and sweeping them off their feet. My interest was pretty innocent; I was wrapped up in the fantasy of "happily ever after." But when my mother found out what I was reading, it was her turn to freak out. She forbade me to read those magazines anymore.

She must have been terrified that those romances would make me boy-crazy and I would end up pregnant. I think she thought that the less I knew the better. Yet if she had told me more it might have been better. The forbidden nature of the topic only made me more curious. So I started hiding those magazines and reading them secretly.

Because our family was dysfunctional and uncommunicative, I began searching outside the home for something more. Although I had a two-parent family, it didn't really seem like that because my Dad was rarely there. When he was, he was constantly yelling at all of us or abusing my mother. It was not a happy time when he was home. I began looking among my peers for the closeness and connection I missed with my family. As a teenager I fell in with a wild crowd. None of us had many positive family influences, so we were all searching for someplace to belong and someone to be with. My friends accepted me as I was, and that was enough to bind me to them, even if they had questionable values.

The kids I hung out with didn't directly pressure me to become sexually active, but their influence certainly sent me that direction—if not through their words, then through their actions. I saw them making out, sitting on each other's laps, touching each other inappropriately in public, and sneaking off to bedrooms in unsupervised homes.

When my boyfriend did begin pressuring me to have sex, it made sense to me to give in. He made it seem like sex was what we should be doing, because that's just what boyfriends and girlfriends did. Aside from the natural call of my hormones, sex offered an irresistible opportunity to be close to someone. I'd never learned other ways to be close to another human being. I'd never witnessed healthy respect or affection between my mother and father.

A couple of my friends got pregnant, but in our group that was also treated as normal and unsurprising. Their pregnancies didn't scare me away from sex—which was too bad. In fact, those pregnancies might even have encouraged me in a small way. Subconsciously, I thought it would make me feel special to have a baby. As a mother I would have a relationship with someone who would belong to me, someone with whom I could share the closeness that I craved.

If only I had felt a closer connection with my family, it might have prevented me from creating those unhealthy connections before I was ready. As I've grown older and started making my own decisions, my siblings and I have grown closer, which has given me a stronger support system to lean on as I reach out to my own children.

If my parents had given me more information about sex, they might also have armed me with some of the social skills I needed to learn: to avoid risky situations, to say "no," and to protect myself. Those kinds of conversations aren't just about giving kids information; they're also about establishing trust and open communication. The conversations parents have with kids about life's difficult choices—like sex—become part of the bonding that helps families feel connected so kids don't need to seek "love" in inappropriate ways. It makes a difference when kids feel comfortable talking to their parents about something they're curious about.

Instead, I knew if I told my parents about something that was happening to me, something I felt or something I did, they would turn it around to appear as if I'd done something wrong: "What did you do?" or "Why are you asking?" They never made any real effort to understand me or my needs. I guess it was easier and more comfortable for them to deflect the blame or to avoid the conversation altogether.

I've worked hard to break that cycle. As a parent, and now as a grandparent, I've tried to open up those lines of communication between the generations. The conversations I had with my kids throughout their youth always had a twofold purpose: to arm them with important information to help them function safely, happily, and productively in a complicated world, and to let them know I'd always be here for them. Of course they always had their share of secrets, and sometimes they didn't want to communicate. That's okay. The important thing is that they've always been able to count on me to tell them what I think they need to know, and to listen to whatever they're willing to tell me.

How did I approach the sex talk with my kids? I don't remember specifics, but I did talk to them, openly and honestly. I explained menstruation to my daughters, so they wouldn't suffer as big a shock as I did. I told them how sex worked, but I didn't leave it at that, and I didn't leave my advice at "just say no." I explained to them why it was a good idea to wait, and openly shared my own cautionary tale with them. They knew I was forced to drop out of high school because I got pregnant, they knew I got pregnant because I made adult choices too young and didn't use protection, and they knew that what led me down that path was hanging around with a crowd that engaged in high-risk behavior.

I told them how I overcame my mistakes and redirected my life so they would understand the importance of learning and growing from their mistakes. However, I also explained how much harder I made things for myself by making poor choices.

I knew communication wasn't a one-way street: I didn't just make speeches, but also encouraged them to ask questions. The conversations weren't always comfortable, but they freely came to me and talked to me more often than I ever did with my parents. My daughters told me about boys they liked, or if someone they knew at school got pregnant.

It wasn't all talk. I knew I needed to also support them with action. I made sure I always knew who their friends were, and insisted they always let me know where they were going. Although they didn't always like the rules I set, the boundaries gave them a sense of security. They knew there was someone at home who cared what happened to them.

Arming them with information, offering a willing ear, and setting boundaries all worked together to create a supportive environment that helped them make better life choices.

I've never been a perfect parent, but I've striven to set a positive example: by getting a good education, by learning to insist on respect from the men I've dated, by being accountable at work, and by making myself accessible as a parent. I've always known my kids were watching and listening, even during the teenage years when they tried to assert their independence by acting disinterested or rolling their eyes.

When parents set boundaries and expectations, it does make a difference. Both of my daughters were fairly responsible young ladies in high school. The elder would sometimes challenge me and rebel, but she followed my rules. In college she began to assert her independence. But because she'd built a strong foundation by then, she never fell too far off course. Both my daughters have had more choices as women because they made smarter choices about sex when they were teenagers. They deserve credit for that, but I also know it helped that they had a mother who helped them understand their options and the consequences.

## Advice from an Expert

To arm you with more information on this controversial subject, let's get the low-down from Dr. Rachel Ross.

Dr. Ross is a sexologist who studies sexuality and treats sexual dysfunction. She has a private practice in Gary, Indiana, where she specializes in couples therapy and child molestation cases. She spends much of her time answering endless questions about sexual health. I ask Dr. Ross why she got involved in a medical field that makes so many people squeamish.

"I grew up in a household where my father was a physician," says Dr. Ross. "My mother told all four of us children that's what we would be—and we all are." But her particular specialty was not a family affair. An unexpected introduction to a dramatic epidemic led her to the subject of sex. "When I first went to college, HIV and AIDS were decimating the white male population. On my spring break one year, I went to New York to work with HIV outreach groups. When I got there, I was shocked to see the sickest people I had ever witnessed. It struck me that it was sex that had got them there, and that piqued my interest in the subject."

As taboo as the subject of sex can be, Dr. Ross finds the broad spectrum that encompasses human sexuality endlessly fascinating. She smiles as she says, "When I was in my residency I furthered my education underneath William Gransik, one of the nation's foremost sexologists. For one project, I interviewed dominatrixes and pedophiles! It's never dull."

If the subject can be exciting, sometimes she wishes people kept the excitement in better perspective. She says sexuality is still an aspect of basic health. And she laments that so many people fail to see sexual health, or their entire well-being, as a continuum. Instead, their lifestyles swing to extremes. "They think, 'If I've got a wedding coming up, then I'll diet for two weeks.' A lot of people overeat because there's this addictive nature to eating that makes it easy to get hooked in the same way that you might on drugs. And sex is the same way. I treat sex addiction regularly."

Dr. Ross also sees a lot of patients with porn addiction, especially men who substitute porn for real relationships. "That often causes problems in their relationships—they expect their wives to perform just like in these fantasy movies. You might have a girl who has been brought up in a conservative way. She wants to please him, but she can't be the porn star. He's not getting turned on and that's the way he needs it. When you're addicted to porn you're training your brain to be turned on by certain things."

Dr. Ross shakes her head, "I'm seeing just porn in general as ruining relationships everywhere. Porn is designed to be entertaining. When you have it in your life on a daily basis it tends to cause dysfunction.

Porn has the same effect on the brain as cocaine does. Our society has made it seem like it is okay to indulge in it, but I see its destructive side every day in my office."

The destructive nature of porn reaches into the lives of children, both directly and indirectly. The Internet has given child pornographers and pedophiles greater opportunities to stalk victims. Meanwhile the Internet, TV, and the entire modern media expose teenagers to more sexual imagery and ideas than ever before. The input is hard for adults to control. It's worse when parents, or trusted adults, become the sexual predators in a child's life.

Dr. Ross says education is the most powerful tool we have to mitigate all these crimes and invasions into our children's innocent world. "The lack of sex education for kids causes problems. It makes them more easily susceptible to molestation. Why? When you think about it, you've got this kid who doesn't know what sex is, so when they get touched, it creates this drive to be touched again."

I ask her what recommendations she has for bringing up children in a world that simultaneously bombards them with sexuality, while it forbids talking about sexuality. She's quick to respond: "Talk to your kids! Girls and boys need to be taught about relationships and the rules. What makes you a respectable young lady or man?"

But you can't just talk to them about following the rules. You also have to talk about what can happen if they don't. Don't dumb down this conversation. Kids know the score. They know what adults are up to, and they're mimicking adult behavior. But sometimes they only know the exciting or romantic side of the story. Give them some gritty consequences to latch onto.

Seventy percent of all Americans admit to having a one night stand. They know this is risky behavior, but how do you persuade them to decrease the risk? The real problem is that sex is all around us. The average age that young urban kids are starting to have sex is between

13 and 14! If you have cable and leave your kids home alone, they are going to be exposed to this stuff long before they are ready. Sex is everywhere. Don't you want them to get information from a reputable source? You need to start talking to them early about sex—in age-appropriate ways, of course.

Teaching kids your values is important, but it's not enough. You also need to give them information on practical back-up plans. This is not a contradiction; it is just an acknowledgment of reality. Why should your child get pregnant, or impregnate someone else, just because you hoped your 14-year-old didn't need to know about condoms? "The reality is that 62% of (sexually active) young women aren't using condoms. The problem is that if you have sex with a condom and then without, the difference in pleasure is night and day. So how do you talk young people into using condoms? You have to treat young people like they are functioning adults. You have to respect that they're making decisions about their sexuality and you need to give them good information. Then you keep your fingers crossed!"

Remember, if you don't talk to your kids about sex, sooner or later someone else will, and it will probably be sooner than you think. "When their buddies answer their questions it leaves out the relationship piece. What they get then is a non-comprehensive sex education—without the emotional connection. That's disastrous. They grow up thinking there are no consequences. It's your job as a parent to talk to them, take away the confusion as much as you can, and help guide their decision making a bit."

Dr. Ross says it's perfectly healthy to talk to kids about sex as soon as they're old enough to understand a simple conversation. You just need to keep your words and ideas simple and age appropriate. "Tell them that they have special areas that no one else is supposed to touch. Then, when they get older, you've already started a conversation so you don't feel as awkward about the situation. If you can make your kid feel comfortable and you feel comfortable, then the discussion comes naturally. You want to try and mold that sexuality. You don't want to traumatize them. It's a delicate issue, but it's not possible to talk about it too much, if you have the right intentions."

I ask Dr. Ross about the controversial issue of distributing contraceptives in schools. You might be surprised to know that Dr. Ross is *not* in favor of it. "Contraceptives in schools is a quick fix. What's really needed is comprehensive education. Children need a deeper understanding of sex as you progress through your life stages. There are so many things young girls, for example, need to learn: how to avoid getting into dangerous situations, how to get out of dangerous situations when you're in them, how to know what's risky and what's safer, and on and on. I don't think they should distribute contraceptives at schools because it becomes an excuse for not offering more comprehensive sex education."

If we want to protect our kids, if we want to help them avoid sexual predators, sexually transmitted diseases, and early pregnancy, if we want them to grow into adults capable of healthy relationships, we can't avoid frank talk. When we explain normal, healthy, responsible sexuality to our children, we begin to deflate the power of the media and their peers to rule our children's behavior. We pull the mask off the excitement and romance, and give them a clearer picture of reality. We give them information that can save their futures and even their lives.

We need to be mentally and emotionally courageous. We have to overcome our reluctance, judgment, and embarrassment. If we want to influence kids to make smart choices about sex, then we have to talk to them about sex. If we don't, consider who will.

# Chapter Six

# Influence Youth to
# Take Education Seriously

*"Education is not preparation for life; education is life itself."*
~ John Dewey

Education is central to success in life, and the United States was once an international leader in education. That's no longer true. The primary role of education today should be to prepare young people to live useful, meaningful lives in the twenty-first century. And a secondary role should be to help our country maintain a competitive advantage in an increasingly global economy. But in too many American cities, for too long, education has not been succeeding at either task.

According to The Alliance for Excellent Education, about seven thousand students drop out *every school day*—that equates to about 1.3 million students every year. And while over one-third of all dropouts occur in the ninth grade, low attendance or a failing grade can identify future dropouts as early as sixth grade. Research shows that a lack of student engagement is predictive of dropping out.

Political leaders, educators, and parents have made many valiant attempts at school reform, yet overall school performance continues to decline in cities around the nation. Money alone is not the problem. Some schools are achieving unexpected success with few funds, while other schools that have received an infusion of cash continue to flounder. So, what is it students need most to help them succeed?

Contrary to popular belief, it's not money, resources, or even human capital. While it's true that we could use more of all those things, the deeper problem is commitment: things won't change until everyone takes personal responsibility for improving education in his community and influencing kids to stay in school. Educators must commit to giving children more complete preparation for their futures, parents must participate in their children's education, and the community as a whole must value education as a priority. In short, everyone must work together to influence youth to take education seriously.

## The Foundation of Our Community

At first glance, it might seem that the topic of education only pertains to schools, students, and parents. However, it's really a community issue that affects everyone, whether they have school-aged children or not. Today's students will be tomorrow's adults, so their decisions and actions will affect everyone at some point. The question is, will the effect they have be positive or negative? The quality of the students' education definitely plays a big part in that answer.

Therefore we need to ask ourselves, "How well is the school system preparing the next generation labor force? How are we going to compete in a global society if our students don't have highly developed skills and talents to offer? With so much blue-collar competition from other countries, how will America's young people carve out a more secure place for themselves in the white-collar market?"

The fact is that public schools must prepare more children to go on to colleges, business schools, and technical schools. Schools also have to pay more attention to the social and cultural development of young people, to prepare them to cope with a more complex society and workplace. It's a tall order but it has to be done, or it means giving up on generations of American children and consigning them to Third World status.

Realize that today's children have to learn a tremendous amount more to be considered educated than their parents did. Ironically, they have to acquire that extra knowledge while bombarded by pop culture images that worship celebrity, material wealth, and a flip attitude toward education. In effect, pop culture is lowering our standards for children precisely when we need to raise those standards, just to stay even with the rest of the world. We need to fight the conspiracy of superstar athletes, half-naked pop stars, and violent video games, with a community conspiracy that strongly celebrates good books, scientific breakthroughs, and intelligent leadership.

The early school years are the time for establishing a solid foundation of basic knowledge and skills for a lifetime of learning. With so much to learn today, even if children fall behind in elementary school, it can be difficult to catch up. They need a solid foundation of basics if they're going to tackle tomorrow's technology.

Students today need to balance the basics, like reading and writing and arithmetic, with new technology like computers and electronics and global communications. The fundamental skills are as important as ever, but the world is changing at an increasingly faster rate, demanding more mental agility from young adults entering the workforce. We need to give them the whole package, and we can't expect to do it at the same cost, using the same ideas, or expending the same energy as we have in the past. The education system must adapt.

How can we make learning attractive to kids today? How can teachers compete with video games, TV, and the Internet? To some extent, they have to recognize "if you can't beat 'em, join 'em," and engage kids in learning via video games, TV, and the Internet. Children can learn how to use the Internet as a fun tool to research and disseminate information. They can play video games that teach them to analyze and interpret information. They can create their own TV documentaries and learn to combine written words with video to communicate stories and ideas.

Yet teachers also have to insist that their students learn to read books, write essays, and solve equations. Those skills will serve them in any field they enter, while the lack of those skills will hold them back. Book reading is still a primary indicator of successful individuals. Even those young people who go into career fields that deal with the modern gadgets they so love will find language and math skills imperative for their success.

Whatever future children want, they must acquire critical thinking skills. There are no shortcuts to that kind of education. This requires not only that children learn, but that they learn how to learn. If we don't teach children to develop a love of learning, they're in for a world of disappointment, because people who live successful lives spend their whole lives learning. People who don't develop the habit of learning will spend their lives at lower income levels, struggling to get by, and unable to comprehend why life is so hard.

Such a total approach to education will take both money and leadership. That leadership needs to come from every level of the education system, all the way from the top leaders in Washington, D.C. to the teacher in the classroom to the concerned adult in the local community.

## Fix What's Broken

Another important key is to evaluate what's working and what's not, both nationally and locally. One of the effects of having 16,000 school districts in the United States without any real central control is that innovations in one place tend not to be replicated elsewhere—the word just doesn't get out. By the same token, programs that aren't working continue to keep popping up like dandelions—the word of the need for weed-killer just doesn't get around.

Innovations that work should be evaluated and shared with similar districts. Programs that have outlived their usefulness should be retired.

Teachers who come up with winning approaches should receive tangible support and rewards. Teachers whose students regularly fail should receive guidance and support to improve their approach, and if their classes continue to fail they should be politely asked to leave. Educational practices that don't fulfill twenty-first century needs should be replaced.

There are still many passionate, talented, dedicated teachers in the system, but they become isolated when the system as a whole doesn't support them well. Many teachers feel discouraged about the possibility for change, because they are already innovators who have seen many efforts at reconstructing education—yet still they are struggling as never before. Many teachers have innovative ideas, but when they're forced to spend half their time on crowd control or on dealing with troubled children, that can derail the best of plans.

It's harder for teachers to exercise discipline than it used to be. Many rules today restrict teachers from using corporal punishment, while many social cues kids receive today encourage them to engage in disrespect and even violence. At a loss for how to discipline kids without using a paddle, teachers sometimes turn to less effective methods. For example, administrators are more likely today to suspend or expel a student for misbehavior. But that only compounds the problem: it forces the child out of the environment that he needs to gain the education, stability, and discipline he needs, and into an undisciplined environment that is more likely to increase bad behavior than to cure it.

Punishing an underachieving kid who acts out in class by kicking him out of school seems counterproductive on the face of it. He's likely to view it as a reward rather than a punishment. Meanwhile, many kids who act out in class have working parents who can't stay home during the day to monitor them. If those kids get sent home from school, they often don't stay home. Out on the streets, they pick up more bad habits and get into more trouble. It's a vicious cycle.

Sometimes the problems that end up in a classroom start in the home. Many students are unable to learn because of bad family situations. They may not be properly fed, clothed, or housed. Certainly those are the responsibilities of parents, not schools, but the reality is that many children don't get the support they need from their families. We need to acknowledge that and respond to the situation with flexibility and vision, or else we will perpetuate a cycle of poverty, underemployment, and despair. Schools must find ways to fill the gap for under-parented children, if those schools are to succeed in educating our future citizens, fellow workers, and taxpayers. That is how public education serves all of us.

We can help break multi-generational cycles of poverty and dysfunction by ensuring that our schools have the internal and external support systems they need to deal with the many issues their students face. When children receive inadequate care at home, schools should do more to connect them with the counselors, social services, health care professionals, and mentoring programs that will help those kids come to school prepared to learn. A school can become a community hub to coordinate a full range of services to make sure that children are able to function fully in society.

## The Influence of Parents and Community

Of course, we also need to reach out and convince parents to become involved in their children's education. Children learn the value of education from their parents. Too many parents have abdicated that duty. It truly takes all aspects of a community functioning together to raise a child. Education is not just a school experience, it's a life experience. Parents must reinforce more thoroughly and consistently what their children are learning in school. Are they getting their kids to read outside of the classroom? Are they taking them to museums and other mentally stimulating activities? Are they exposing them to other cultures?

Too many parents have the attitude toward educators: "You deal with my kid. I'm a busy person. Don't bother me." Too many educators won't admit the extent of the problems in their schools. Neither of these attitudes is acceptable. As with most of the world's problems, we can't expect the world to change unless we are willing to change as individuals. The solutions must not only come from the topdown, they must also come from the bottomup, from the classroom, from the home, from every member of the community.

When it comes to education, our idea of community must include businesses. One of the functions of education is to prepare today's children in the classroom to become tomorrow's leaders in the workplace. So educational leaders need to coordinate with local and national companies to ensure we're providing the level of education and training that businesses expect from tomorrow's workforce. What good will it do our kids if they have a top-notch education, but none of the skills required to obtain a real job?

Corporations can do their part by supplying expertise and materials that meet the standards of the twenty-first century. Corporate leaders are easy to involve in educational partnerships: they know full well that it's in their best interests to contribute to building a well-trained pool of employees from which they can draw in the future, and they know it's good public relations to support the needs of children in their community.

These professionals can help teachers show students how the things they're learning in school can relate to their futures in the real world. Such involvement can greatly enrich the quality of education for children at a critical juncture in their education. The more connected children feel to their education, the more likely they'll stay committed to that education through high school. This is a tool that can ultimately help to reduce the dropout rate.

I was fortunate to go to school in Gary when it boasted one of the best school systems in the country. At that time, a generation ago, people came from across the U.S. to visit and study Gary's schools, to see how they might replicate our success in their hometowns. As I recall my childhood memories of school, what stood out overall was the feeling that I was important to my teachers, and that my teachers were important to me.

Like many urban school districts around the country, Gary is no longer the model for success it once was. But this is not the time to give up; it's the time to recognize a perfect opportunity to try new ideas. The first step to reclaiming the tradition of excellence in educational systems across the country is to be honest about the extent of the problem, to get excited about change, and to commit to a new direction. No matter what direction we take, I believe one memory from my childhood still answers the primary need that all good education programs will fill: the need for committed teachers, strongly supported by the community.

## Outside Learning Opportunities

Although we typically think of learning as occurring primarily in the classroom, we often forget that children learn just as much, if not more, outside the classroom. It does a child no good to have a parent send them to school with the expectation that it is solely the responsibility of the school to educate our kids. Unfortunately, many adults are under the assumption that when we send our kids to school, it is the teacher's/school's responsibility to educate them and to teach them to be model citizens. We forget that it is first and foremost the parent's responsibility to help establish a solid foundation, consisting of behavioral and academic expectations.

This is why it is so important for adults to help impress upon students the importance of education, and to influence the learning that takes place inside and outside of the classroom, so we can channel the experiences of these young people in a positive direction.

Parents are usually the first teachers, followed by the family and the environment in which the child spends her time. One great way for parents to model the importance of education is to volunteer time in the classroom. If that's not possible due to job and time restraints, parents can take on projects, such as fundraising initiatives that help teachers to purchase necessary supplies and materials for learning. Additionally, they can join the PTA and attend school board meetings. These types of activities show kids that educational concern and involvement are important.

Also realize that outside learning opportunities abound. Some examples include:

- Spend time at the library exploring the world of books. Children not only learn to read, but by taking out a library card, they learn responsibility for borrowing and caring for the property of others. Bookstores can also be a good resource.

- Go on nature tours. This is good for any age. Visit a state park. Go for a hike. Observe the many species of birds, other wildlife, trees, and plants. Discuss how your part of the country may be different than others in terms of what it has to offer.

- Go for a walk on the beach. Collect shells. Take them home and research pictures of them to identify the various types of shells found.

- Encourage your children to help you cook in the kitchen. Teach them how to read recipes and measure ingredients. Take the time to teach them the various measurements. This helps with math and reading skills.

- While driving, have your children read road signs and billboard advertisements to you. This helps them to not only improve their reading ability but also the speed at which they read.

- Read the newspaper with your child. Select current events and discuss them, particularly issues that might be interesting to the child.

- Visit museums. These are always great places to learn about science, industry, history, and geography.

- Visit zoos to learn about various animals and their habitats.

- Visit your local city hall or state legislature to learn about government and politics. If you are comfortable with it, older kids can volunteer to assist with political campaigns to learn how the democratic process should work. They can also serve as pages during the legislative session by contacting their local representative and making the request.

- Get involved in sports activities. These are not only fun and healthy, but they teach the importance of teamwork.

- Plant a garden. Gardening is a way to teach science and have fun learning about the environment.

- Go to harvest festivals to learn about farm animals, agriculture, and the types of produce grown on farms.

- Listen to different types of music to teach music appreciation and appreciation for other cultures.

- Go to a planetarium or use a telescope to learn about astronomy in a fun way.

- Play with Legos or blocks to learn how to construct or build projects.

- Put together a puzzle to build mental acuity and problem solving skills.

As you can see, learning is always happening…and it need not be a bore! Get to know what your child is interested in and find a way to make a fun and educational activity around it. The more engaged your child is, the more likely he is to value the importance of education.

## Influence in Action

To illustrate how profound an impact influence can have on a child's education, consider the story of my husband Chuck, a firefighter who helped "light the fire" under a young person and get him interested in school again.

One day, Chuck and a fellow firefighter were having a slow day because of a snowstorm. They decided to go the local fitness center to work out and play basketball. Because of the storm, no one else was in the facility. Shortly after they arrived, though, two young teen boys came in.

Chuck and his friend challenged the teens to a game of two-on-two basketball. The older guys prevailed, and as is typical with guys, they started to brag and trash talk to the youngsters.

The smaller teen, JC, indicated that he could play better than he had in the game. Chuck dared him to do so. He did…and played remarkably better. At about 5'10" and 140 pounds, JC displayed lightning quickness and a vertical jump that allowed him to dunk the basketball with two hands. Immediately Chuck asked him what school he played for because of his remarkable skill.

JC revealed that he had dropped out of high school. Chuck then asked him if he were a "hoodlum" or a "thug." JC resented the remark and quickly added that he quit school to care for his invalid father. That turned out to be somewhat true in that his mom had deserted the family and left him to live with his dad who was, indeed, disabled. JC had apparently honed his basketball skills by not going to school and spending hours in the gym playing basketball.

Chuck saw the potential in JC and took him under his wing. After a while they developed a mutual trust and, with some convincing, Chuck got JC to agree to go back to school, be a good student, stay out of trouble, and play basketball. At the time, JC was 17 years old. Therefore, under Indiana High School Athletic Association (IHSAA) rules, he was only eligible to play basketball for one year. During that one year, he impressed many college coaches. However, academically and because of his poor attendance, he was only classified as a sophomore and could not pursue the scholarship offers made to him.

Both Chuck and JC were devastated. The thing that had convinced JC to go back to school was basketball. Keeping him encouraged and interested in high school was going to be a challenge without his having the ability to play on the team.

Through some research, Chuck found a junior college in Kansas that would let JC enroll if he passed a GED. JC took the test and passed. But as a result of his academic history, he had to sit out of basketball for one year. He used that time to focus on his studies. After the first year, he played for the college basketball team for two years. And because of his great skill on the court, he had a number of scholarship offers to attend almost any college or university of his choice. He ultimately received a scholarship to the University of Hawaii where he was a standout performer for the two years he attended. JC currently resides in Hawaii where he is gainfully employed and not a dropout statistic.

Having been an athlete in high school and college himself, Chuck was able to use his knowledge and experience with athletics and academics to impress upon JC the importance of going back to school. He was able to influence him by using the thing that JC loved and was good at—basketball—as a hook. Because he took the time to find out what JC's situation was, he was able to intervene and get JC the assistance and resources he needed to get moving in the right direction.

## Embrace the Future

As we evaluate our nation's schools, we don't want to become slaves to numbers. However, numbers do provide us some basis to begin to evaluate whether a school is performing competitively or is ripe for a change. So as we evaluate a school, we do need to consider how that school's students perform on standardized tests. An even more important number is the teacher-to-student ratio.

Beyond numbers, we need to ask the basic questions. Are class textbooks adequate or antiquated? What kind of modern technology is readily available? How actively are the PTA and other organizations involving parents and teachers? If a school is doing poorly, these are a few obvious indicators of where changes might be needed. If a school is doing well, these are a few items that other schools can begin to emulate, to kick-start the process of change—so long as there is public will to find the funds.

All parents and adults need to be informed consumers of education. Find out how the schools in your district are performing. It's time we hold schools and school administrators/officials accountable for the performance of the schools.

In seeking to improve our education system, while change is necessary, we don't need to waste time reinventing the wheel. We can start by finding the great teachers, programs, and schools that already exist. We need to celebrate them, emulate them, and reframe them to fit the individual needs of our many communities.

We must keep our minds open to new and unfamiliar ideas as well, to shake up our thinking so education can become as innovative as we want our leaders of tomorrow to be. The world is changing rapidly and we have to change our approach to education to keep up with the faster pace of modern communication, ever-changing technology, and an increasingly global marketplace. If America is to remain competitive, we must give our children the support they need to take us there.

## Chapter Seven

# Influence Youth to Stop Violence

*"The main goal of the future is to stop violence.*
*The world is addicted to it."*
~ Bill Cosby

Our children have disappeared. We woke up one day and noticed they were gone. When did that happen?

Was it when drugs became epidemic in our communities? No, that wasn't a cause, but a result.

Was it when metal detectors became features of our schools? No, that wasn't a cause, but a result.

Was it when rap music began to glorify violence and hatred of women? No, that wasn't a cause, but a result.

So, when did our children disappear? The answer is simple: when we stopped listening to them.

Adults today often treat their kids like little grown ups, and expect them to act that way. That's not what children need. Treating kids like adults is sometimes the result of a well-meaning intention to show children that we value them, to treat them as partners in our lives, and to teach them the survival skills they'll need in the adult world. But it is possible to do all those things without forgetting that they are children, and that they deserve a childhood—with all its mistakes, limitations, and awkwardness. Children need to learn from their mistakes, find protection from damaging mistakes in the limitations we set for them, and discover their true selves through the experimental process of "I don't yet know how to act, what I want, or who I am."

It's good to respect our children as equal partners in our world, but we don't need to dress them like grownups. It's good that our children know we are willing to share things with them and want them to share things with us, but we don't need to talk to them like grownups. It's great that we offer them the opportunity to grow through taking on new challenges, but it's unsafe and unwise to pretend that they're ready to deal with grown-up problems.

Sometimes even when we try to establish clear boundaries between adulthood and childhood, our children still try to assert grown-up independence beyond their years. Some of that is a natural desire to enjoy the fruits of a world that seems forbidden, or a natural desire to grow to the next level. Unfortunately, some of that is also because the modern world is filled with so many images, opportunities, and dangers that compete with parents, schools, and community authority for control of our kids. In this fast-moving, multifaceted world, sometimes children feel pressure that they can no longer afford to be children. There are too many temptations they want to give in to, or too many dangers they need to protect themselves from.

## Let Kids be Kids

Because we know how much is lying in wait for our children out there, sometimes we feel we can no longer afford to let them be kids. Sometimes adults want to give them more information about the big bad world than they're prepared to understand, in hopes that this information will somehow prepare them to better protect themselves. Sometimes adults think they have no choice but to give their children up to that adult world, because it's too hard to fight the tide. Sometimes we get so scared of that big bad world that we ignore it completely and try to hide children behind a wall of fear and ignorance. That's how today's children often get the worst of the adult world and none of the benefits; it's also how they get the worst of being kids and none of the benefits. This is why we must give childhood back to our children and influence them to stop the violent behavior that dominates the media.

Unfortunately, we can't turn back time. It's never going to be like it was a generation ago. The sad reality is that we do need to protect our children in ways our parents never did. We do have to prepare our children for a world that is in some ways grimmer and uglier than it was. We do have to provide for our children in a world that is simultaneously filled with more opportunity and more uncertainty than ever before. We have more opportunity in terms of technology, knowledge, and interconnectedness; we face more uncertainty in terms of jobs, family, the future of our economy, and the future of our planet. Both opportunity and uncertainty are double-edged swords, because both present a dizzying array of choices and risks, many of which children are not mentally, physically, or emotionally prepared to face.

As hard as it is in complicated times, if we are parents, mentors, or teachers of children, then it is still our job to lead them…and it's their job to follow. It is healthy for them to ask questions and push boundaries. In fact for most kids, especially teenagers, testing the limits and pushing the boundaries is normal. Kids try to determine just how far they can go and what they can get away with, so they test the waters. It is a sign of growing up and figuring out just who is paying attention and how much they will be able to get away with.

But until they're adults, we must be the ones with the answers, not them. Until they're adults, we must maintain those boundaries, only widening them as we see that they're truly ready. There will be plenty of time for them to be grownups. Let's not rob them of their childhood. If we do so, we could actually damage their adult lives, because childhood is a time to prepare for adulthood. You would not climb a mountain without training first, or you might fall off a cliff. Don't let our kids become adults before they've done their childhood training, or they might fall off a cliff and land in early pregnancy, unemployment, crime, or just aimless living without purpose.

Here are a few things you can do to help children hold onto their childhood, even when your family, your community, or your nation is facing the toughest of times.

1) **Prepare kids for adulthood little by little.** Introduce them to the grown-up world in small doses. There's no rush: 18 years is a long time. They should take baby steps from a smaller, safer world of tight rules and discipline into a bigger, scarier world of greater responsibility and freedom of choice.

   Treat the realities of life the way teachers treat the difficulties of math: show kids the easy stuff first, then gradually introduce them to the harder stuff. Most students can't learn trigonometry or calculus until they've progressed through basic math, algebra, and geometry. Most children won't know how to avoid the wrong crowd as teenagers if we don't insist on knowing who their friends are from the time they're small. Most children won't have the ability to say "No" to drugs if we haven't spent time talking to them about what drugs are and the consequences of drug abuse. Most children won't know how to steer clear of violence in the streets if we don't teach them conflict resolution at home.

   We can't let this training wait too long, always thinking, *I'll have that difficult conversation tomorrow, or next week, or next year.* You want to wait until they're in middle school? Or high school? In some neighborhoods, drug dealers are selling to kids in elementary schools, sixth graders are carrying knives to school, and junior high kids are carrying guns because they're afraid of other kids in gangs. Don't wait until you're comfortable, or until the time is perfect, or until the age that you *hope* these issues will come up. You will be too late.

2) **Make it clear that you're the adult and they're the children.** Most teenagers, at some point in their youth, do engage in risk-seeking behavior. They seem to enjoy the excitement and challenge of pushing boundaries. They want to push their parents' buttons to get a charge out of them or just to see if they can get a reaction.

Too often adults fail at these tests because they have difficulty separating the role of being a child's friend from being the responsible adult or parent. Parents often find themselves trying to be their child's friend out of fear that the child will be upset, or not like them if they punish them, or make normal demands in terms of behavior and expectations. Kids view friends as persons who are on their same level with no authority over them. Therefore, parents who opt to be their child's friend often put themselves in a situation where the child has no respect or appreciation for them in their role as responsible adult.

By clearly establishing yourself as the parent, you set the expectation and clarify the role that each of you play in the relationship. As the parent, you must set rules and establish consequences for when the rules are broken. If the rules are broken, parents must not hesitate to enact the appropriate discipline. Children who are not disciplined feel they can get away with just about anything and they will continue to push the boundaries, often ending up in more trouble as their behavior gets worse.

Therefore, set limits for your kids, your students, or the children in your care, even if they grumble—and they will. Demand that they follow the rules you set down, clarify the rewards they'll receive if they do, and the consequences they'll suffer if they don't. Then make sure that the rewards are real and dependable, and that the consequences fall on them like gravity. You need to be strong for them, to protect them from the world and to help them prepare for the world.

3) **Provide role models for them and a safe environment for them by getting your own life in order.**

Children learn incredibly fast, and they learn by example. If they come home to violence, drug abuse, promiscuity, or irresponsibility, that's what they'll learn. Children who are victims or witnesses of violence often become either perpetrators or chronic victims of violence, which affects the next generation, who go on to become perpetrators.

If abuse or dysfunction exists in your home, or in the home of a child you know, your awareness of the problem is a first step to breaking the cycle. If you can accept that you need help, then you can reach out your hand and break the cycle. If you can accept that a child you teach or mentor needs help, not condemnation, then you can reach a hand out to her. When people become aware of the possibility of change, it becomes easier to accept the need to change. Only when people accept the need to change will they take action to change. And when people take action to change, they *do* change.

For example, my friend John McKinley recently told me his experience with helping a young gang member change his ways. The boy, who went by the nickname Grease, grew up in a low income poverty area. He lived in a single parent home where his mother struggled to raise eight children alone. His mom was having difficulty managing the children and trying to give them the guidance they needed.

By the time Grease was 12, he was involved with a gang and started skipping school. He also began committing petty crimes, such as breaking into homes and shoplifting. He eventually started dealing drugs to earn extra money. At one point he was shot by a rival gang member. However, the injury was not life threatening and did not deter him from his street life.

When Grease reached high school, in spite of his poor attendance and poor grades, he briefly participated on the football team. Unfortunately his football career was cut short due to his unwillingness to conform to the rules, which required him to attend practices regularly, not miss school, and earn passing grades. He quickly gained a reputation as a troublemaker and a person who would probably spend most of his life behind bars.

In the community, a Midnight Basketball League had started. The league was based on the premise that getting young men age 18-26 off the streets, and providing them an avenue for structured activity during the hours that they would most likely be committing crimes (9 p.m. to 2 a.m.), would benefit both them and the community at large.

Grease heard about the program, and although underage at 16, he showed up one night to participate. John, the league organizer, described Grease as brash, disruptive, precocious, and disrespectful of authority. However, John saw this as a smokescreen, a false sense of bravado, in a young man who was virtually spending most of his time on the streets and in bad company. He saw that underneath the pretense was a very likeable but misguided young man, and he decided to allow

Grease to stay and participate in the league. John's rationale was that the only alternative was to release him to the streets where he would be wreaking havoc on the community.

John spent time during the league hours getting to know Grease and finding out just what motivated him. He eventually became a mentor of sorts to Grease. He talked to him frequently about personal responsibility and about what he needed to do to continue to participate in the league, including how he should behave during the hours when he was not in the gym.

Slowly Grease began showing signs of improvement, maybe because he was finally getting the type of guidance he needed or perhaps it was simply due to having a responsible male in his life. Whatever the reason, Grease stopped getting into trouble. He eventually quit his gang involvement and started attending school more regularly.

Today, Grease is gainfully employed. He also is a minor partner in a small business—a sports bar.

With the intervention of John, whose influence made a significant impression in Grease's life, this young man has certainly defied the odds.

## When Good Turns Bad

Sometimes, despite our best efforts as adults, a good kid can mess up and start to veer on the path of questionable behavior. Does this mean the child is doomed to a life of chaos? Of course not. We all make mistakes from time to time. The key is to catch the behavior early and make swift changes in how you influence that child to get back on track. Some suggestions include:

- **Keep your kids on a schedule.** What time do they go to bed and wake up? Do they eat at scheduled times during the day? How do they fill the hours in each day? Are they involved in structured activities? By keeping your kids busy, they can't get into trouble because they don't have the time nor do they get bored enough to look for activities to entertain themselves.

- **Communicate openly, honestly and regularly with your children.** In doing so, they will be more likely to trust you and to go to you with their problems. Also remember that timing is everything. Try not to approach them when you are angry or busy. It's easier to start these conversations at times when things are relaxed, positive, and going well. It is at times like these that they are more likely to open up and share what's on their minds with you.

- **Be willing to negotiate.** As parents, we have a tendency to want to tell our kids what to do. We expect that our kids will go along without question. But "Because I said so" is usually not an answer that kids accept readily. By discussing with them what you'd like to have happen and allowing them to present options, you may avoid feelings of resentment and rebellion among your young charges. You may also encourage thoughtful deliberation and critical thinking skills in their young minds. Understand that in the process of negotiation, they may not always live up to their end of the bargain. This is normal. The negotiation process should include consequences for irresponsible behavior and an understanding of how to earn continued privileges by showing responsibility.

- **Set limits.** Kids often appear to resent restrictions placed on them. However, if you begin setting limits when they are young and if you do not deviate from your expectations, they will begin to accept that you mean business and will be less likely to attempt to undermine your authority as they get older. Establishing who's in charge and setting limits are key components of shaping and influencing youth behavior. It is our responsibility as adults to provide the guidance and discipline that young people need to get them off to a good start and to keep them on the right track. This is not always easy.

Ultimately, if children experience nothing but chaos, violence, and neglect, that's what they'll learn. But if instead they experience order, discipline, and kindness—they'll learn that. If you put in the work to create that safe, loving environment, they'll repay you by making you proud, and your life as a parent will ultimately be easier.

And your children won't disappear.

## An Inside Perspective

Mike Prendergast, Special Agent for the FBI in Indiana, knows where the children who disappear end up. He's seen a lot of them in his line of work. I visit with Mike to ask about the causes and effects of violence against children and violence by children. He has had a front row seat to that answer: first, during his youth in Chicago, where he grew up around gangs and had personal experiences with them, and second, during his 30 years with the FBI. Although Mike received training in accounting, he ended up doing crime work. You could say it was his calling. He's worked on it all: white collar crime, violent crime, organized crime, and even terrorism.

"Since 1990, I've been in the northwest Indiana region, working on gangs and violent crimes," he says. "We merged our gang response teams with the violent crime and drug units in Gary to respond to the crack cocaine epidemic that was fueled by the gangs. Ten or fifteen members of a gang would take out a whole neighborhood. Drugs, violence, and robberies—it wasn't pretty."

Listen to Mike, and you'll begin to understand why it's important to ensure that children have a childhood. Those who don't, often grow up into childlike adults who never develop a healthy respect for themselves or others—including their parents.

"Most drug lords live with their mothers," Mike says. "That's their base. They have a second house where they do their illegal stuff. They use their mother's address for their legal activities."

Hopefully, most of the people reading this book don't have a drug-dealing son or daughter living in their homes. So I ask Mike what the average person should be worried about when it comes to these kids who grow up to become gang members and criminals.

"Unfortunately," Mike says, "in some hard-up neighborhoods in the cities, the gangs gradually take over. They give out money to kids to be (drug) runners, and to keep watch on the street corners. Gradually, everyone gets sucked into the gang life. Remember, if you're, say, 10 years old, and some well-dressed older person is giving you money and telling you you're cool for doing not much, that's very seductive. And the kids may not be getting much positive reinforcement from anywhere else. This makes it hard to combat the gangs block by block."

So how do we fight back and influence kids to stay away from this world of violence?

Mike responds: "Schools are the best outlet, if you can keep the kids there from 8:00 to 3:00. When I was a boy, I attended a Catholic school. I knew that if I got in trouble there, I would also be in trouble at home. That's really important. The kids need to know that there's consistency from home to school. In way too many families in the inner city, that's just not the case. The kids get more love, more attention, more money—and Michael Jordan shoes—from the gangs. They don't get that kind of attention at home. That's the heart of the problem."

Mike says the seductiveness of the gang life has grown over the years, while the fear of consequences has decreased as kids have become desensitized to violence. "Materially, the gangs can provide so much. And guns are everywhere. It's nothing for kids these days to be shot or stabbed. They don't think twice about it. It doesn't scare them off. So they see the easy life on the one hand, and the hard slog of going to school and working honestly for a living on the other. It's not much of a contest, I'm afraid."

I wonder if the state can do anything to fight the trend. Mike paints a pretty discouraging picture of the failure of existing programs. "These are kids who are familiar with the system from the inside. We pick up kids nine or ten times, but they're in and out of juvenile detention so fast it doesn't affect them. The system is overcrowded and under-funded. Kids are just cycled through. They go back to their value system of drugs and crime, and that's what they learn. The girls get thrown into the welfare system because they get pregnant and become young mothers. They actually get money for having kids. If we could change the system, we could perhaps have a shot at changing the cycle of poverty, gangs, drugs, and violence. But it won't be easy. For many of these kids, starting at a very young age, it's a way of life."

Although Mike sees the system as failing, he knows some of the changes that could turn failure into success. "There has to be effective communication between enforcement and prosecution. We need a real police presence in schools, so that we can help the kids that need help. And we need more alternatives besides incarceration. They're not all bad kids. You can turn some of them around."

But creating that turnaround requires the leaders of our country to honestly accept that the system is broken, to listen with open minds to suggestions from those on the ground, like Mike, and to take whole-hearted action with an eye toward real change.

Until that happens, Mike can only give advice to parents whose children still have a chance: "Be familiar with your kids," is Mike's most important suggestion. "Spend time with them. Be involved in their schoolwork and know who their friends are. If you're aware of some of these things and you've set down rules, things are going to go better. You've got to trust kids, but you've also got to lay out consequences. You have to be supportive, honest, and open. If you just yell and scream at them, you'll isolate them more. And be prepared to be tough. If you think they are doing stuff, bring home a drug test. If you've got worries, talk to them. Worry about your kids and the influences on them. Talk to them about drugs and sex. These shouldn't be taboo subjects. If you're afraid to talk to them, they're going to learn it from the streets. Which do you think is better?"

Mike also offers advice that can be tough for some parents to hear. If you want to be a strong parent, he suggests that you have to accept the possibility that it's not just other people's kids who are bad influences. All kids have the capacity to screw up, even the good ones… even yours. "Know who your own kids are influencing," Mike says. "If you've got kids coming to your house younger than your children, figure out what they're up to. Do they spend a lot of time on the cell phone, texting? Watch their access to the Internet."

But even when you suspect your kid is getting into trouble, Mike says it's important to maintain the integrity of your family relationship. "Tell them up front what you're going to do," Mike says. "Don't sneak around. As hard as it is, you've got to be honest with them. Bottom line is that you've got to treat kids with respect. They will respond in kind."

Special Agent Mike Prendergast understands the delicate balance between the need to treat kids like kids, at the same time that we let them know we value them as important members of our family and community. Only by staying closely involved in the lives of our children can we combat the violence that threatens all of us, but especially threatens them. We must insist that our children listen to us, because we really do know best. But we must also listen to them, because only they know everything that's going on in their lives, and if we don't listen, we'll never know.

## Chapter Eight

# Influence Youth to Rise Above Failure

*"Failure is the foundation of success,*
*and the means by which it is achieved."*
~ Lao Tzu

It's an essential part of the human experience to realize that all of us fail sometimes. Equally important is that each of us has the ability to pick ourselves back up and move on, if we choose. Success is a matter of perseverance. When you stumble, you have to redirect your focus and keep heading forward. In fact, it's your responsibility to do so. It's your responsibility to yourself not to sell yourself short, it's your responsibility to your community not to make other people pull your weight when you know deep down that you're capable of more, and it's your responsibility to today's youth to show them how to rise above failure and pick themselves up.

Of course, the best way to overcome failure is to focus on and encourage success. As a parent or other concerned adult, you certainly want the best for the children in your life. The natural question that arises is, "How do I best help my kids navigate the world and encourage their success?" One of the challenges to answering this is that everyone's view of success is different.

For some parents, a son who brings home B grades is highly successful, while others see the grades as falling short. The fact is that the way your child experiences success is largely dependent on whether he feels successful—right now.

For instance, if your son brings home a B-average grade report and you say, "This is good, but you can do better next time," he may feel like he let you down and didn't succeed. If he's like some kids, who are motivated to please their parents, this may be the catalyst he needs to push harder and raise his grades. But if not it may have the reverse effect, causing him to give up, thinking, "What's the use? I'll never be able to make them happy."

Ideally, you'll foster a natural desire for success in your children and provide them with guidance to know when they are doing well and when they need to improve. Developing this natural desire happens through one key attitude: acceptance.

When you can accept your child, wherever she is right now, she will learn that success doesn't come from external circumstances or forces. Instead, success comes from inner peace and self-confidence. Of course, this means you will likely re-evaluate your biases and opinions about what defines success for you and your children.

As you begin to explore a new definition of success, consider these ways you can begin to nurture a child's natural desire to succeed, on terms that increase their confidence and resilience—two necessary attributes in today's frenzied world:

- **Celebrate your child's accomplishments.**
  There's always a reason for celebration with children! Acknowledging their accomplishments in genuine, open, and fun ways helps them feel successful. When you or another significant person in their lives appreciates their unique talents, skills, and gifts, their success barometer rises.

- **Accept your child as he is—today.**
  It is vital that you accept your children as who they are rather than who you want them to be. You want the best for your children, but don't let that desire turn into disappointment

when they fall short (in your opinion). Kids are tuned in and know immediately when they fall short of your expectations, and this affects their motivation and self-esteem.

- **Give your child's talent time to develop.**
  It's hard to avoid comparing your child to other children. Comparison begins at infancy when the doctor gives you the weight and length of your new baby. It's news that you publicly share. Friends and family say, "Oh, he's so big and healthy!" But not all kids are born "big and healthy." It takes time for some kids to develop physically, mentally, and emotionally. Support and encourage your child at every level of his or her development and watch your child's sense of success grow.

## The Three P's for Success

Of course, despite your best efforts at encouraging success and helping the child feel successful, failures will occur. They're inevitable in life. But failure never means everything is lost.

Sometimes overcoming failure requires reshaping your priorities. But you're never a failure at life just because you make mistakes that force you to change course. In fact, making the necessary changes to turn failures into opportunities is an essential ingredient in any success story. The task is never insurmountable: if you can envision change, you have the power to make change.

In fact, the failures we make on our way to a goal can teach us much greater lessons than the successes. Sometimes it's only by learning what not to do, that we clearly see what we must do to get where we want to go.

Unfortunately, we live in a microwave society where most expect to get what they want – instantly, or at least in less than a minute. We're tricked into believing that fame and success can be achieved overnight, if we'll only work harder, longer, and faster. We've adopted an "all or nothing" attitude that says we must either succeed or fail, there is no in between. But there is an "in between," the period between success and failure that for some, lasts for years. Let me share with you a brief story.

Patty was a young girl who came from a broken home. By the time she was in middle school, she was constantly in trouble with the law for stealing and fighting. At age 16 she dropped out of high school, spent her days with the wrong crowd of kids, and soon became addicted to cocaine and heroin. Having no way to pay for her drug habit, she turned to prostitution and became pregnant not once, but twice.

Due to her lifestyle and situation she was unable to care for her children, so she left them with her sister to raise. I wish I could say that Patty cleaned her life up soon after that, but she didn't. In fact, she remained a drug addict and prostitute for nearly 20 years!

She hit rock bottom after being arrested and sentenced to jail for stealing from a department store to feed her drug habit. Ironically, while Patty sat in jail, her sister worked on the other side of the bars as a correctional officer. Since Patty now had a lot of time to think while in jail, she made the decision to clean up her life once and for all.

Once she was released, she tried hard to live a "normal" life. She attended Alcoholics Anonymous meetings, worked at a halfway house as a substance abuse counselor, and took a job selling vertical blinds. She even reestablished communication with her two children and returned to high school (as a student) with her son. It wasn't easy balancing her new life, but she did her best, took her time, and eventually graduated from high school.

But Patty's newfound success didn't stop there. Realizing how good it felt to work hard and be productive, Patty continued her schooling and earned both a bachelor's and a master's degree. Today she is working toward her Ph.D. in counseling. Now that's what I call moving from failure to success!

I hope you and the children in your life aren't facing a situation like Patty's. Her experience is definitely extreme. But if someone like Patty can go from failure to success, so can you.

To help youth navigate that period between failure and success, keep the three P's in mind:

### Passion

Do you have a passion? What is it and how can you express it more fully in your life? If you consider yourself to be "passion-less," then I suggest spending time looking back on your life to see what excited you in the past. Your passion may be lying in wait, hoping you'll see it.

Likewise, do you see any passions developing in your children? Do they love art, math, writing, music, soccer, baseball, dance, science? Even a focus that seems "frivolous" to adults, such as computer games, can be a worthwhile passion to help your child develop. A love of computer games, for example, can lead to a lucrative career as a game developer, computer programmer, or technology innovator. Don't squash or dismiss a passion simply because you don't understand it. Find the positive in your child's passions.

### Positive Perspective

What is your perspective? If circumstances are not exactly as you had hoped, are you tapping into your passion to turn it around, or wallowing in negativity? Although external factors may not be ideal, your internal perspective can be just what you need to make it better. You just have to choose to think differently.

Model for your children the belief that any situation can be seen in a positive light. Share your own setbacks and stories of how you turned it around with the proper perspective. Remember, perspective is something you develop, not always something you're born with.

Focusing on the positive of a situation is a habit you practice and develop. Teach your kids how to adopt this healthy habit.

### Perseverance

Most success stories are actually years in the making. Nothing good ever happens overnight. Chances are high that at some point your child will experience a setback. It may even take several attempts to reach success. That's normal and okay. Perseverance is key.

So don't give up. Success could be just around the corner. Keep in mind that "slow and steady wins the race." I learned this when I trained for my first marathon. It took time and baby steps to build the endurance and fitness I needed to run 26.2 miles, but I persevered. Today, I have six marathon medals.

These lessons are as much for you as they are for the children you influence. Share these success ingredients with the young people in your life. But more important, teach them that popping these ingredients into a microwave doesn't mean instant, ready-in-a-minute success. Show them that the "in between" is just as important as the achievement.

## Find Success with Goals

One great way to help kids achieve success and rise above failure is to influence them to create goals. I'm a firm believer in goals. The adage, "You must conceive it to achieve it," is a belief that still inspires me to pursue bigger dreams every day.

Although goal setting is a commonly known activity, it's not commonly practiced, especially among our youth. Most kids think about what they want, but few translate that into an actionable plan that gets them the results they expect.

The good news is that goal setting is a learned habit that you can teach a child, and it's as easy as answering these simple questions (asked and answered from the perspective of a child):

1. **What is a goal?** A goal completes the sentence, "I want to…"

2. **Why is setting a goal important?** Goals show us what's possible. They give us something to shoot for. They're exciting!

3. **How do I know a goal is good?** A good goal describes exactly what you want, when you want it, and why you want it. For example, "I want to advance to the next level in reading by my birthday because I know my mom will be proud of me."

4. **How do I achieve my goal?** Set a plan! Imagine you're at the bottom of a ladder and your goal is at the top of it. What steps do you need to take to move up each step of the ladder?

5. **What if I fail?** It's okay! Goals usually stretch us to do more than we've ever done before. If you miss a goal, think about what you learned and how you might approach it differently next time.

As you help your kids develop and write out their goals, show support but don't take over. Let children come up with their own goals and action plans. Let them own their goals and they'll be more likely to achieve them and experience success.

Teaching children how to plan ahead and set goals provides life skills that will help them thrive as adults. It's also a great opportunity for you to reignite your own dreams to achieve goals alongside them. After all, what better way to influence children in this new skill than to do it yourself?

## Navigating the Pitfalls

Few people have an easy life that's free of failure. Like most people, I have had to stand up to people who didn't believe in me, overcome failure, and find a support system. I have failed more than once on the way to success. And I was raised in a family with low expectations.

When you're growing up, it's hard to be certain about who you are if you're surrounded by pain and confusion. It took me many years to realize I was raised in a house of failure. My father never did achieve much, nor did he really want to. He felt more comfortable as a victim, blaming *The Man,* or the *Powers That Be,* or anyone he could think of, for all his problems and his lack of success. Blaming others gave him an excuse for not trying. His doomed-to-fail attitude negatively affected everyone and everything around him.

For us kids, it meant hard times. We wore hand-me-downs that were one step above rags. We put cardboard in our shoes to cover the holes in the soles. We had no indoor toilet.

Failure was what was expected of us. It was the very air we breathed. If we won little victories in life, like a good report card or a kind word from someone on the block, my dad would ridicule us. "You think you're smarter than everyone else?" he said. Or, "You think you're better than everyone else, don't you?"

When we wanted kindness, we got sarcasm. When we needed guidance, we got indifference. When we gave him honesty, he gave us rage.

I've wondered many times why I didn't just pack it in like Dad did. He'd made it clear that failure was an easy option, not just for a girl but for us all. I saw our poverty as a failure. I saw my father as a failure. But there was a kind of comfort in that word: failure. Failure tells us that all we have to do is give up and our struggles and strife will all be over.

But I didn't lose faith. Instead, I've used my father's failure as a motivation. And his insults no longer have power over my life, except as a lesson in what not to do. I've been able to do this because I've been blessed with a strong sense of self.

That gift came from people like my mother, my grandmother, my first grade teacher Mrs. Kaufman, and my oldest sister: people who told me that I was intelligent, talented, and giving. I chose to believe them instead of my father. They taught me to never ever apologize for my natural gifts. Strengthened by those voices in my head, I fought back. I knew I wasn't stupid. I was determined to prove my father wrong.

Those people also taught me the importance of being a similar source of inspiration and empowerment to the young people I now come in contact with in the field of mental health services. Many of them hear a lot of negative messages in their lives, pushing them toward failure. But you never know which positive messages might be the extra push they need to send them the other direction, toward success.

It's not as if I turned my failures into success overnight. As I grew up there were times when my father's voice took over, and times when, in spite of the other positive voices, I still made big mistakes. When I was in high school, my thick skin and strong sense of self made me feel powerful! Unfortunately, I thought that was all I needed. Soon I fell in with the wrong crowd. It was round-the-clock party time. I was the cut-up, the sarcastic one. My friends and I had fun, and not much else.

My bad behavior drove my father around the bend, which was an added bonus for me. If he didn't like it, then I knew I surely did. The social group I chose for myself at 16, as fun as it was at times, was nothing but a grab bag of party favors: fun for a while, but pointless and soon broken. Nobody spoke of dreams or aspirations. Whatever any of the other members of the group wanted to do, well, that was fine with the rest of us. You want to stay out past curfew? No problem! You want to skip class and hang out with your friends? Go for it!

The biggest problem was that no one challenged anyone else in the group. Under that influence, I soon stopped challenging myself. I drifted from moment to moment, from party to party, all the while digging my hole a little deeper every day. Without intending to, I had recreated my home life all over again. Just like before, failure was everywhere I looked.

Soon enough, the joke was on me. I made the biggest mistake of my life: I got pregnant while I was still a teenager. With that, I found myself kicked out of school and discovered that my friendships only lasted as long as the good times. Yes, I had a first-rate sense of self, and I was the proud owner of a leathery hide, but I was still missing a key ingredient for successful living: I hadn't yet learned from previous failures how important it was not to give up after getting knocked down—or knocked up—even if the person who knocked me down was me.

I didn't want to drop out of high school. Even though I was pregnant, I would have stayed in school if the system had let me. But there was stigma against pregnant girls in high school. The school board, administration, parents, and students all adhered to the accepted notion that pregnant girls would be a disruption in school.

There was still a chance for me, if only I would recognize that I needed to make some changes in my life and seek alternatives, or else face the direst of consequences. I now had my own baby daughter and my own bills to pay. I began to look for work.

I remember reading the descriptions of jobs in the want ads and saying to myself, "I know I can do that job!" I met people who did those jobs and they weren't any more capable than I was. They did, however, have one requirement for the job that I didn't: a high school diploma. All of the passion and purpose in the world wouldn't get me any of the jobs I wanted, not without that diploma.

It was fear that motivated me to go back to school and get my GED (General Equivalency Diploma). Fear isn't all bad, so long as you allow it to motivate you instead of paralyze you. I didn't want to be labeled as a person who was incapable of focusing on a goal and making it happen. I had a need to see something through. So I did.

Fortunately, although my high school's administration had kicked me out, my teachers had given me a solid educational foundation up to the point when I left. That foundation stood me in good stead. When I took the GED test, I got the highest score anyone had ever achieved in that district. The program director told me that with my scores, I should go on to college. He said my job prospects would greatly improve with higher education. But at first I just wanted to get a job so I could start supporting my daughter and myself.

I quickly found out the ugly truth behind the program director's words. Even with my GED, the only job I could get was working for the bedpan brigade at the local psychiatric hospital. I was furious! It was degrading. I had to clean up after patients who sometimes smeared feces on the walls, and worse.

Instead of feeling grateful to have a job and considering my alternatives to work toward a brighter future, I was again tempted by my father's voice. I started to give up and blamed the world for my lot. I perpetually showed up late, did as little as I could get away with, and showed a sour face to the world.

I still remember the day my supervisor told me, "You're always angry." She was right. Nothing was good enough for me, and nothing was ever going to get any better. That attitude was setting me up for more failure. At first the anger made me feel righteous and powerful, and living in constant conflict with the world relieved my pain like a drug. But, like a drug, the anger ultimately left me isolated and empty. I spent so much energy on my rage that I had no energy left for laughter or love, and certainly no energy to consider what I might do to get myself out of this situation. Luckily, my supervisor's words penetrated my hardened exterior, and I was smart enough to take them to heart and make the choice to change myself.

I still felt angry, but instead of taking my frustration out on my work, the people around me, and myself, I decided to put my anger to constructive use. I transferred all that negative energy into setting and achieving some new goals. I knew I didn't want to clean bedpans for the rest of my life. At the same time, I saw teachers, nurses, and doctors working in that hospital. I saw the respect they commanded, knew that they earned better pay, and sensed that their jobs gave them a sense of purpose. So I resolved to fight my way into their world.

I enrolled in classes at the local university. At first I didn't have the goal of earning a degree. That was too much to contemplate. But I knew that more education would improve my chances at better employment. Then, when I did well in my first few classes, I registered for more. I began to see that each class could become a stepping-stone to a bachelor's degree. I began to believe I could do it, if I just moved forward one step at a time.

## A Foundation for Life

I think growing up poor was what steeled me to deal with the hardships of attending school as a poor, single, working mother. When I was a child we didn't have means, so we learned to make do. As an adult I called on that experience again, as well as ongoing support from my mother and grandmother, who had always told me, "You can do anything you put your mind to." Sometimes the oldest sayings are the truest, and now I was finding out the most important part of that aphorism: it's meaningless until you act on it.

It was a struggle going to college with a baby. When I started going, I was 19 or 20, and I was afraid I was going to be the oldest person there. But when I got there I found that the diversity of people in terms of age and race was amazing. I wasn't anywhere close to the oldest: people 50 and 60 years old took many of the same classes I did.

Being a working mother with one child, and then two, would have been a challenge in any case. But for a student it was the challenge of a lifetime. Yet, once again, I learned that what looked like a recipe for failure had within it the seeds for success, because juggling life as a mother, student, and employee forced me to become very skilled at time management. I also struggled financially, but this made me skilled at money management. Both those skills, along with many others I learned, would be of great service to me in my future career.

I often had to work twice as hard as other people to get what I wanted. But I had learned the hard way that wasting time on self-pity would not change that. Step by step, I struggled forward to each finish line I set for myself.

I had help along the way: a cousin who had gone to college, a couple of helpful counselors in school, and the chairman of the department where I was an undergraduate, who hired me and encouraged me to go on to get my master's degree.

There were also people who tried to become stumbling blocks in my life, who tried to drive a wedge between me and my belief that I could succeed. I needed that belief to keep me moving toward success. But I didn't let their discouraging words penetrate my thick skin, another skill that would help me stay on the road to success for the rest of my life. There are always people who want to see you fail, or who take the opportunity to remind you of the failures and obstacles of your past. Beware their clever manipulations: they will tell you that your belief in yourself is arrogant, that your desire for a better life surrounded by like-minded people is traitorous to the people from your past, that your drive to succeed is unrealistic. If someone talks down your success, that's their own self-esteem issues talking, their desire to feel better about themselves by pulling you down.

My grandmother always used to say, "Don't be concerned about others' opinions—don't make their problems your problems. If they can't deal with the fact that you are going to college don't make that your problem. Continue to strive toward what it is that you want to do." It was great advice from a great lady. She died in 2002 at 95, but she lives on in my head, and so do her words. Her voice still gets me through difficult moments with difficult people and keeps me on the path to success.

The day I got my bachelor's degree was a big milestone for me. The whole family showed up. I was the first one in my immediate family to earn a college degree.

Little by little, I had turned failure into success. And having learned from that experience, I now understood that this was a gift I could draw on again and again: I knew that I could reinvent my life at any turn. So, with my degree in hand, I decided to redefine myself as someone who mattered. The truth is that I mattered all along, just as everyone does. I just had to open my mind to the lesson that all of us have the power to turn failure into success.

My key to success was simple: I never gave up. But remember, "never" is a one-day-at-a-time proposition.

"One day at a time" is the motto of twelve-step programs like Alcoholics Anonymous. Those programs, and that motto, have helped save millions of lives. In my career, I've sat across the desk from many people I never thought could quit drinking or break a drug habit, and then had the privilege of watching them do just that. The key to finding the inner courage and resolve to turn around the downward spiral that was ruining their lives was in that motto: one day at a time. They set small goals, and moved toward them inch by inch, day by day.

I've also seen people fail who I thought had all the right stuff to break a habit. They invariably had one thing in common: instead of accepting that change is a day-by-day process, they tended to look at their fight as "All or nothing." So they ended up with nothing.

If you set forth only two options for yourself, total success or total failure, you're headed for a train wreck. That's like trying to get your bearings in unfamiliar territory by looking in all directions at once. It gets quite disorienting. Failure loves it when you set huge, overwhelming goals and try to tackle them in one fell swoop. Instead, set small, interim goals that will carry you toward your ultimate goal. Those small goals should feel real, ordinary, everyday. They should require small steps you feel confident you can make, one day at a time.

In a culture with an all-or-nothing attitude, sometimes we forget that the greatest success stories are always a long time in the making, with many failures along the way. This is not only true in recovery programs, but in all aspects of life.

## Choose Success

Whatever success means for your child, help him or her realize it's unrealistic to expect too much too fast. On the other hand, don't let children sell themselves short, either. Help them realize they can't let other people define who they are, just as they can't let failure define who they are except insofar as it helps reshape them for success.

As your children strive for success and work to overcome failure, influence them not to give up at the first stumbling block, roadblock, or blockhead move. They will have setbacks in life, period. There's no way around that. But a setback is not the end of the world; in fact, it could be the beginning of a new direction for their lives. It's certainly worthwhile for them to take a look at what went wrong and decide how to approach things differently in the future. As long as they believe in themselves and keep moving past failure, they can accomplish anything.

Sometimes people—especially children—limit themselves by not opening themselves to what life can teach them. This is where your influence is priceless. Show them that criticism, rejection, and failure are things you can overcome—they're only frightening until you've lived through them. Help them see that sometimes you have to try in spite of your fear, or else you'll never know what you might have accomplished! And when failure is staring you in the face, you need to avoid the temptation to blame others or to blame yourself. Help children recognize what went wrong, take responsibility for their part, work with other people to improve their part, and then use the lesson they've learned and move on to success.

The final influence lesson for your kids is this: The choice is up to each of us—accept occasional failure and achieve success, or insist on all-or-nothing and live a life of failure. Success is a choice. It's a choice you, and you alone, can make. Don't worry; you're more than enough. So go for it! Choose to turn your life around, and take it in the direction you've always wanted. If you think about it, it's really the only choice worth making.

# Chapter Nine

# Influence the Future Today

*"You don't have to be a 'person of influence' to be influential.*
*In fact, the most influential people in my life are probably*
*not even aware of the things they've taught me."*
~ Scott Adams

Today's youth are our future and, as such, they need people to influence them to take the right path. Contrary to what many people believe, it's not completely up to parents to influence children, nor is it completely the task of teachers. It's up to everyone to shape the future generation so we all have a future we want to live in. Remember the old saying, "It takes a village to raise a child." You're a member of that village too.

Whenever I urge parents, educators, and community members to step up and be a positive influence to youth, I often hear responses like, "Why me?..." "I can't..." and "That's not my role..." I beg to differ with all those replies. In fact, I'm going to debunk the top five responses right now.

- **I'm not the right person to influence a child.**
  You may feel like you just don't know enough to offer any true wisdom or direction to anyone. Or maybe you feel as if you need to achieve a certain level of success before you can impact a child. If so, you may be working under the false assumption that you need to know everything (or you need to have a "perfect" life) to give advice to others. In reality, you're steps ahead of someone and have valuable insights and experience

to share. Remember, even if you're only one step ahead of someone, that's okay. You can still share something valuable.

- **No child would ever listen to me.**
  You may be right. Not all kids will listen to all adults, at least not at first. This is when you must expand your definition of what influence is. It could be a big role, such as being an advocate or advisor to youth. Or it could be a smaller role, such as setting an example. While you may not have the patience to interact with youth, you may be well suited to offer periodic advice or live a certain example. Don't feel you must fulfill every aspect in a child's life. Start small and do what you can. Over time, a real relationship can evolve and more can be added down the road, if it feels right.

- **I don't have time for this.**
  Your life is already full. Every day you juggle demands at work and at home. It's hard to imagine having time for doing anything else. But influencing needn't be a formal process where you meet face-to-face. In fact, some of the best influencing takes place casually and in creative ways. Texting a positive message, sending a positive email to a child, or even just saying "hi" on the street can be enough to show a child you care.

- **I don't know any kids.**
  Young people today are hungry for someone to guide them, teach them, and support them. Make a conscious effort to seek them out. You can reach out to your personal network or get in touch with a variety of nonprofit organizations that are actively seeking volunteers. Some organizations to consider are Big Brothers Big Sisters and Boys and Girls Club

of America. Or check out VolunteerMatch, an organization that helps match your interests to a volunteer opportunity, like mentoring.

- **I'll end up giving more than I receive.**
  Forcing your influence on someone can feel burdensome, leaving you feeling depleted and used. Neither party should feel exploited. That's why it's important to establish clear boundaries from the outset. When you do, you'll find the payoffs of being a positive influence to be well worth your efforts. You'll feel a sense of contribution and purpose and you'll feel a greater sense of confidence in yourself when you see the positive impact you have on others.

With a new perspective, you'll find that taking the initiative to influence youth can benefit both you and the child. You'll impart wisdom to others and gain new insights for yourself.

Realize, too, that being a positive influence isn't just about leading the way. It's about developing a child's natural talents and abilities so she can become a mature, contributing, and productive adult. Yes, it takes time to teach a child the life skills she needs to succeed, but you will ultimately help produce a confident, self-reliant child who is ready to take on the challenges awaiting her in today's tumultuous world.

Also, keep in mind that you don't have to go full-bore all at once. **Take baby steps.** I've seen parents throw their kids in the deep end of the pool as a way to quickly teach them to swim. Of course this approach may work for some, but generally, it's not effective. When you're interacting with and trying to influence a child, start small. Set initial expectations low and build from there. Small wins have a snowball effect, building momentum and growing through consistent forward action. Allow your child to experience the joy and satisfaction of success.

Then, increase the challenge little by little, giving her room to grow and gain confidence.

Additionally, kids learn by doing and observing. An effective way to teach a child a life skill is to model it in action, and then invite the child to participate. For example, literacy and communicating through writing are necessary skills for children and adults. For a child learning to read and write, you can spend time reading with or alongside her for 15 minutes every day. Another idea is to write your child a short note, help her read it, and ask her to write a note back. The key is to model the way, teach the way, and then allow your child to get involved.

Finally, when you're interacting with a child, it's hard to resist the urge to just do it for him. A child learning to tie his shoes seems to take forever manipulating the strings. You're impatient and ready to walk out the door so you grab the shoestrings and quickly do the job. The shoes are tied, but your child is left feeling inadequate and frustrated. As a parent and person of influence, it's important to give children the freedom to make mistakes and come up with their own solutions. At the same time, allowing them to flounder and struggle for too long can have a negative effect. Instead, look for the balance between freedom and floundering. It's different for every child, so be aware and observe the shift in attitude and behavior as your child tries new and challenging skills.

## An Intentional Approach to Influence

It's often too easy to overlook the effect we have on children. We tell ourselves that children are resilient. They are more malleable, so if they see us screw up they'll get over it. But let's not take that belief too far.

Children are watchful beings and they soak up everything they see like thirsty sponges. So while our behaviors and actions may not have an immediate effect on them, there is an effect (even if it comes to full fruition much later in their lives). That's why striving to be a positive influence is so important.

Of course, we can't be perfect. That's impossible and striving for perfection is unhealthy. Instead, I suggest taking an intentional approach to influence. It's an approach that ramps up your self-awareness so that you're not living life with blinders on. Instead, you're consciously making choices that not only enable your success, but also enable the success of the children around you.

Intentional influence involves:

- **Being proactive.** Being proactive means more than responding to issues before they become problems. It's really about taking personal responsibility for your beliefs, actions, and behaviors. Teach personal responsibility to children by demonstrating it yourself.

- **Having a dream.** What's your dream? Ask a child and he'll excitedly tell you his wild, fanciful aspirations. Yet for most adults, dreams were lost years ago. You must have a vision and keep the ones in children alive. Dreams give hope, and we need more of that.

- **Aligning priorities with values.** Most of us have a personal moral code that informs our actions and behaviors. But some times, external pressures push those values away. We react rather than respond, teaching children to do the same. It's important to first, know what you value most, and then consistently act in a manner that aligns with those values.

- **Looking beyond our own needs.** We ask children to share all the time, but rarely put the needs of others ahead of our own (at least in a genuine way). In every interaction, seek ways that produce a "win" for all sides. It's not always easy. It takes more time. But it's a lesson in humility and understanding we all need more of.

- **Filling accounts.** In his book *The 7 Habits of Highly Effective People*, Stephen Covey introduces the idea of an "emotional bank account," where we each make deposits and withdrawals from our relational accounts with others. Actively seek ways to fill the accounts of others, and don't forget to fill your own account; it's important to replenish yourself.

Ultimately, intentional influence is about being conscious and awake to the effect we have on the world around us, and the children in it.

## Yes, YOU Have What it Takes to Be a Positive Influence!

In my personal and professional life, I've been privileged to be on both the receiving and giving sides of influence. Those experiences have allowed me to see the characteristics of great influencers. Here are the top seven characteristics I've seen in people who do the most good. Chances are, you already exhibit many of these traits.

1. **Great influencers are credible.**
   You don't need to be a personal answer book to a child. You don't need to "know everything." All you need is to be credible. If you know an answer, great. If not, you probably know how to find it or where to lead the child. A great influencer has credibility to guide youth in the best direction.

2. **Great influencers have a positive point of view.**
   It's tough to respect a person who is a bad role model. Great influencers are aware of their individual impact on

others, or how their behavior and actions affect those around them. When a person is positive, objective, and upbeat, it's much easier to trust and learn from him.

3. **Great influencers show genuine interest.**
   Let's face it. It feels good to have someone take an interest in you, and great influencers know this. They don't take an interest in people out of obligation or responsibility, but because they genuinely want to help. It's this level of passionate interest that drives the most successful relationships.

4. **Great influencers openly share what they know.**
   Storytelling has long been the way people have communicated through generations. It is through stories that influencers share their experiences, insights, and knowledge. They freely offer their personal stories as a means for others to develop their own.

5. **Great influencers ask great questions.**
   Most would agree that open-ended questions are best. Instead of asking, "Did you have a good day?" an influencer will ask, "What was the most exciting thing about your day today?" Influencers look for more than the surface answers. Instead, they seek meaning, values, and purpose in what you say because that's where the catalyst for a child's success lies.

6. **Great influencers offer fresh perspective.**
   Objective feedback is a key benefit of having someone influence you. A great influencer offers a new spin on your old ideology because she doesn't live it every day like you do. She offers a distant clarity that you're missing because you're too close to a situation.

7. **Great influencers listen empathetically.**

   Listening is such an underutilized communication skill, but great influencers don't take it for granted. Instead of leaping into problem solving, they listen—with their hearts first, and then their minds. They know that problems are often resolved by the simple act of listening because ultimately, influencing isn't about them having the answers. It's about helping you discover your own.

## Make Your Move

In my day-to-day role as CEO of Edgewater Systems, I see the positive impact that the right influence at the right time can have on the lives of the community members we serve, and the employees I help lead.

I've seen former drug addicts radically change their lives and then give back by guiding a desperate addict to sobriety. I've seen seasoned social workers willingly support interns as they learn to navigate a mental health career. I've even seen children function as influencers when they urge a peer to "do the right thing."

What I've learned from these experiences, and my own personal journey, is that no one is "self made." Everyone needs some positive influence to truly succeed in life. And if you think about it, the need for influence makes perfect sense. We are designed to be relational beings. We exist to be in relationships with others. We feel better, we do better, and we are better when we're connected with others. And that's the foundation of influencing youth.

Sadly, today's culture has become increasingly individualistic. We cling to personal independence and self-sufficiency when we really need interdependence and meaningful relationships. We've exchanged community participation for individual super heroes (you name it, "super mom," "super student," etc.) who save the day.

Don't get me wrong, I believe strongly in personal responsibility and the need for individuals to take charge of their lives. It's a foundational part of my own success. But we need a balanced approach, one that involves both personal responsibility and involvement from others. Beyond this, we must make it acceptable to say, "I need help," and remove any negative labels associated with needing support.

The bottom line is, everyone needs someone. Whether you call it a mentor, a friend, a sounding board, or a concerned adult, it's important to build those connections to enjoy a positive future. The need for positive influence is even more critical for young people, who face challenges today that I couldn't have imagined when I was a child.

Yes, I'm passionate about helping young people. I hope reading this book has sparked a bit of passion in you too. Be a positive role model and a person of influence today. Today's youth need *you*.

# Acknowledgments

I would like to thank the many people who helped me to write this book. First and foremost, thank you to my parents and my grandmother Daisy—you provided the inspiration for the ideas and concepts presented in these pages. I owe a special thanks to my husband, Chuck—you have always been there to encourage my every endeavor and to provide the feedback that keeps me grounded. Thank you to my children, Lea, Kyla, and LaVeta—I so appreciate your unwavering support. To my first grade teacher, Mrs. Gussie Kaufman, I extend a special "thank you"—your early influence helped me to build upon the lessons you taught me and to hopefully pass those on to others.

There are many people who consented to be interviewed and/or lent their stories to the writing of this book to whom I am grateful: Dr. Steve Simpson, Dr. Rachel Ross, Special Agent Mike Prendergast, and Brandon Freeland. To each of you I say thank you for your passion and commitment to "influencing the future."

To the Edgewater Systems team—I am regularly inspired by your understanding and commitment to showing how it is possible for all kids to succeed given the positive influences that help them to flourish, even in the most challenging of circumstances.

Finally, to Dawn Josephson, your insight and ability to help me clarify my message was immensely helpful. I owe you a true debt of gratitude for what is now the finished product.

# About the Author

$W$ith an amazing story of transformation, hope and triumph over difficult odds, Danita Johnson Hughes is a healthcare industry executive, speaker, author and entrepreneur. Through her professional work, keynotes, writing and philanthropic activities, she inspires people to dream big and understand the role personal responsibility has in achieving success.

As a high school dropout and unwed teen mother, she was the statistic that many considered doomed for failure. Refusing to give into her circumstances, Danita made a decision that changed her life: she decided to take personal responsibility for her situation and turn it around.

She earned both a Bachelor's and Master's degree in Public Administration from Indiana University Northwest. Continuing her education, she earned a second Master's degree in Social Service Administration and a graduate certificate in Health Administration & Policy from the University of Chicago and finally a Ph.D. in Human Services from Walden University in Minneapolis. Armed with education and hope, she set out to change her life and the lives of those around her.

Today, Danita is dedicated to helping people of all walks of life establish and achieve lofty goals as the President and CEO of Edgewater Systems.

She lives in Valparaiso, Indiana and is married with three daughters.

# I'd love to speak at your upcoming event.

I deliver fully customized, 30-60 minute keynote presentations on the following topics:

- Personal responsibility
- Leadership
- Women's issues
- Mentoring

I have spoken in a variety of venues and for audiences that include educators, women's groups, leadership classes, women prisoners, and civic organizations. I prefer to do paid keynotes. However, I reserve a portion of my speaking schedule for no-fee keynotes for fledgling, non-profit organizations.

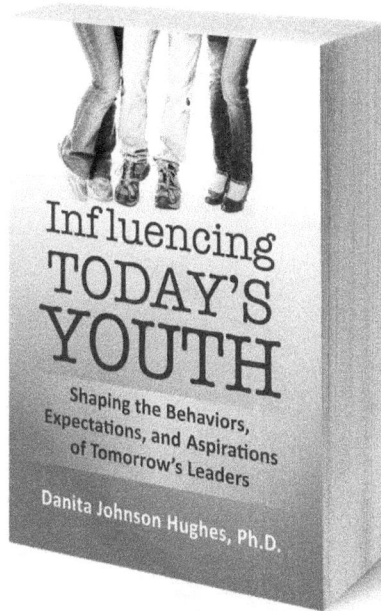

Influencing TODAY'S YOUTH

Shaping the Behaviors, Expectations, and Aspirations of Tomorrow's Leaders

Danita Johnson Hughes, Ph.D.

If you are interested in having me speak at your next event, please contact me with the following information and I will get back to you as soon as possible:

- Type of speaking engagement: paid keynote or no-fee presentation
- Title of event and theme
- Date and location of event
- Audience demographics and size
- List of other speakers and topics

To schedule a speaking engagement or for more information, please contact me at **info@danitajohsonhughes.com**.

To purchase additional copies of this book, please visit my website at **www.danitajohnsonhughes.com**

www.ingramcontent.com/pod-product-compliance
Lightning Source LLC
Chambersburg PA
CBHW020906090426
42736CB00008B/508